Interpretationshilfen

Gran Torino

Cornelsen

Gran Torino · Interpretationshilfe

Erarbeitet von Patrick Charles

Verlagsredaktion
Neil Porter

Umschlagdesign
Heike Börner, orangerie grafikdesign

Umschlagfoto
mauritius images/alamy stock photo/CTK

Technische Umsetzung
L101 Mediengestaltung, Fürstenwalde

www.cornelsen.de

1. Auflage, 1. Druck 2018

Druck: AZ Druck und Datentechnik GmbH, Kempten

ISBN 978-3-06-036358-2

PEFC
PEFC/04-31-2260

PEFC zertifiziert
Dieses Produkt stammt aus nachhaltig bewirtschafteten Wäldern und kontrollierten Quellen.

www.pefc.de

Contents

To the student 5
Technical details 6
Clint Eastwood: director and actor 7
Reception 14
Synopses 21
Characters 35
Structure, genre and style 55
Camera work, editing and soundtrack 63
Themes, imagery and symbolism 68
Setting and context 102
Written test 118
A brief glossary of cinematic terms 126

To the student

Gran Torino is an enjoyable film, with its combination of emotional drama, shocking action and occasional comic relief. It is intended to be a serious but entertaining film. It is an unpretentious film which tells its story clearly and carefully.

When you approach it as a film to be studied, you can take a similar approach to any other text (play, novel, poem): watch it at least once just for itself – to enjoy it, to familiarize yourself with its "shape", and to get a feel for how the story develops, who the characters are, what the film is about (beneath the story – its themes). Then you can start looking at isolated bits of it – individual scenes, for example, or patterns running through the film.

When studying a film you have new things to consider: why does the camera focus on this person now? Why is this music playing? These factors do not make the business of analysing a film any more or less difficult than studying a book: it just means that you have to look at different things. Think of the camera and the actors as tools the film uses to tell its story: just like the style, language and tone a writer uses, the elements and possibilities of cinema are devices and techniques used to share a story and ideas with the audience.

The film is set in a place (de-industrialized Detroit) and time (the financial crash of 2008) which has relevance to the world of the film. Context is important here: not to be able to understand the story and its emotional impact, but for a deeper grasp of what kind of an environment the story takes place in. Issues of immigration and religion are also important. This study guide provides some basic background information on the relevant context.

In this study guide you will find:

- Concise summaries of the film, scene by scene
- An introduction to the director and main actor, Clint Eastwood, brief details on the technical details, a glossary of cinematic terminology and an overview of important background information
- Breakdowns of the structure of the film
- A systematic presentation and discussion of the characters
- Analyses of the film's themes, imagery, symbolism and the techniques used to tell the story
- A written test

Technical details

Released: 12 December 2008 (USA) / 5 March 2009 (Germany)
Running time: 116 minutes
Age rating: 12
Budget: $33 million
Box office: $270 million

Filmmakers

Director: Clint Eastwood
Written by: Dave Johannson & Nick Schenk (screenplay)
Produced by: Clint Eastwood, Bill Gerber & Robert Lorenz
Cinematography: Tom Stern
Editing: Joel Cox & Gary D. Roach
Music: Kyle Eastwood, Michael Stevens & Jamie Cullum
Shooting location: Detroit

Cast

Walt Kowalski – Clint Eastwood
Father Janovich – Christopher Carley
Thao Lor – Bee Vang
Sue Lor – Ahney Her
Mitch Kowalski Brian Haley
Karen Kowalski – Geraldine Hughes
Ashley Kowalski – Dreama Walker
Steve Kowalski – Brian Howe
Martin the barber – John Carroll Lynch
Tim Kennedy – William Hill
Vu – Brooke Chia Thao
Grandma – Chee Thao
Youa – Choua Kue
"Spider" (Fong) – Doua Moua
Smokie – Sonny Vue
Trey – Scott Eastwood

Clint Eastwood: director and actor

Nothing exists in a vacuum, least of all pop culture. *Gran Torino* is a late entry in the decades-long career of one of the most famous and iconic figures in American cinema, and it deals with many of the themes and ideas he has been interested in throughout his career as both an actor and a director. It is therefore recommended to take a look at who this man is and what he has achieved in cinema.

Biography

ddp images/Joe Camporeale

Eastwood was born in San Francisco, California on 31 May 1930. He had a comfortable family life and began working in film in the 1950s. In 1971 he began directing films as well as acting in them. He has had major successes throughout in his career. In each decade he has managed to star in and/or direct films which have had a large cultural impact, as well as being successful at the box office. Eastwood has become an iconic figure in American cinema, and has been extremely influential throughout his long career.

Two of Eastwood's children were involved in the film: his son Kyle wrote the music, and his younger son Scott plays Trey, Sue's boyfriend.

Eastwood's career in film

Clint Eastwood began working as an actor in the 1950s. He played small roles in different projects for several years before finding success for his portrayal of a cowboy in the popular TV Western series *Rawhide* in 1958.

When *Rawhide* ended in 1965, Eastwood managed to make the jump from television to film when he took the lead role in the Italian director Sergio Leone's Western *A Fistful of Dollars* (1964). This was one of the first and most famous of what are now called Spaghetti Westerns (Westerns made by Italians and filmed in Spain). Eastwood and Leone made two more Spaghetti Westerns together, the others being *For a Few Dollars More* (1965) and *The Good, the Bad and the Ugly* (1966).

Eastwood plays a character known as The Man With no Name, a grim, mysterious, cigar-smoking antihero who moves through a very dark and unforgiving world, much more violent and morally troubled than the traditional cinematic world of American Westerns.

After the commercial success of these films with Sergio Leone, Eastwood continued to act in Westerns, but also began to work in other genres: *Coogan's Bluff* (1968) was a violent cop thriller and *Where Eagles Dare* (1968) was an epic adventure set during World War Two. He even appeared in a musical, *Paint Your Wagon*, in 1969.

In the 1970s Eastwood continued to appear in Westerns and war films, including important films like *High Plains Drifter* (1973, which he also directed) and *Kelly's Heroes* (1970). A major turning point in his career came in 1971 when he starred in and directed the psychological thriller *Play Misty for Me*. This was the first time in his career that he had full artistic control over a project, and the film was a commercial and critical success.

But the major landmark of his career in the 1970s was the Harry Callahan character he played in *Dirty Harry* (1971), which was followed by four sequels: *Magnum Force* (1973), *The Enforcer* (1976), *Sudden Impact* (1983) and *The Dead Pool* (1988).

Harry Callahan is a tough cop in San Francisco who is determined to see justice done, by any means necessary. The character is a vigilante cop – he commits morally and legally questionable acts of violence against criminals but is nevertheless a police officer. The first *Dirty Harry* film includes the famous line "Are you feeling lucky, punk?" when he threatens a criminal with a gun. The films celebrate guns, violence and vigilantism without reflecting on the negative sides of these themes. Some critics thought the films were fascistic at the time, and they have remained very controversial because they appear to present a positive image of vigilante gun violence. The character of Harry Callahan, like The Man With no Name, has become a cinematic icon, and has to some degree influenced Eastwood's career ever since.

In 1978 he made the comedy film *Every Which Way But Loose*, which was extremely popular: it was his most commercially successful film up to that point, despite being such an unusual genre for an actor famous for his grim and tough roles. He made a sequel, *Any Which Way You Can*, in 1980.

Eastwood continued to be successful into the 1980s and continued to try out different genres. His 1982 Cold War action film *Firefox* was a huge success. Other popular and successful films he made during the 1980s include the dark psychological thriller *Tightrope* (1984) and the buddy comedy *City Heat* (1984). However, he remained interested in the Western genre, making *Pale Rider* in 1985. This film was based on the 1953 film *Shane*, one of the most famous and important Westerns of all time. *Pale Rider* was a great commercial and critical success, and Clint Eastwood began to be treated with more respect and to be taken more seriously as a filmmaker.

From the late 1980s on, Eastwood moved away from larger projects and began to explore his more personal interests. This included the film biography *Bird* (1988) about the jazz musician Charlie "Bird" Parker and *White Hunter, Black Heart* (1990), which was a film about the real film director John Huston and the filming of Huston's classic *The African Queen* (1977). These films were failures at the box office.

In 1992 Eastwood made one of the most important films of his career, the Western *Unforgiven*, about an old gunslinger and killer who has given up a life of violence to become a farmer, but who is forced by circumstances to pick up his guns one last time. This film is very important because it looked at the classic gunslinger hero which Eastwood had become so famous for portraying, but focussed on new themes: What happens when cowboys get old? What does a life of violence do to a man? It was seen by many critics as an attempt by Clint Eastwood to look back on his own career – in both Westerns and in ultra-violent action films like *Dirty Harry* – and also to reflect on the classic themes of violence, heroism, masculinity and courage in American cinema. *Unforgiven* is an important film in the history of the

Western, American cinema and Eastwood's career. It is also very interesting as it provides some context for *Gran Torino*, which looks at many of the same themes, with a similar maturity, but which focusses on a main character who is now even older, literally at the end of his life.

Unforgiven firmly and finally established Eastwood as one of Hollywood's most important living filmmakers. He continued to make films which were hits at the box office and popular with film critics, including the political thriller *In the Line of Fire* (1993), the thriller *A Perfect World* (1993) and the romantic drama *The Bridges of Madison County* (1995).

In the 2000s – 50 years after he began his career in cinema – Eastwood was still regularly making films which were commercial and critical successes. *Mystic River* (2003) was a very dark crime thriller about sexual abuse and won two Oscars.

Another major film was the sports drama *Million Dollar Baby* (2004) about a female boxer, which won four Oscars and is considered to be one of his masterpieces.

In 2006 he made two war films about the same battle in the Pacific during World War Two, *Flags of Our Fathers* and *Letters from Iwo Jima* – the first was told from the American perspective, and the second was about the same events, seen from the Japanese perspective.

Gran Torino was released in 2008 and became the most commercially successful film of his career to date, making more than $268 million at the box office around the world.

Eastwood continues to make films in his 80s: his film *Jersey Boys* (2014) about the pop group Frankie Valli and the Four Seasons was based on the Broadway musical of the same name and was a huge hit. He continued to be interested in war, making *American Sniper* in 2014, which was based on the autobiography of an American soldier who killed 225 enemy soldiers during the Iraq War, and found it impossible to leave the war behind him when he returned to civilian life.

Eastwood's most recent film is *The 15:17 to Paris* (2018), about the true story of three American citizens who find themselves caught up in a terrorist plot on a train in France. The film was not successful at the box office and was reviewed very negatively by film critics.

Awards and nominations

Here is a brief selection of some of the awards Clint Eastwood has won for his work in film during his more than 60 years as an actor and director. His films have won literally dozens of other prizes from national, regional and critical organizations and institutions. The specific awards for *Gran Torino* are listed in the chapter in this study guide on Reception (p. 14).

Academy Awards (Oscars)

Best Director for *Unforgiven* (1993)
Best Picture for *Unforgiven* (1993)
Best Director for *Million Dollar Baby* (2005)
Best Picture for *Million Dollar Baby* (2005)

Blue Ribbon Awards (A Japanese prize awarded by film critics)

Best Foreign Language Film:
The Bridges of Madison County (1996)
Mystic River (2005)
Million Dollar Baby (2006)

César Award (France's national film prize)

Best Foreign Film:
Mystic River (2004)
Million Dollar Baby (2006)
Gran Torino (2010)

Directors Guild of America

Outstanding Directorial Achievement in Motion Pictures:
Unforgiven (1993)
Million Dollar Baby (2005)

Golden Globe Awards (awarded by the Hollywood Foreign Press Association)

Golden Globe for Best Director:
Bird (1989)
Unforgiven (1993)
Million Dollar Baby (2005)

People's Choice Awards (an American TV show recognizing pop culture, voted for by the public)

Won Favorite Motion Picture Actor and Favorite All-Time Motion Picture Star: 1981, 1984, 1985, 1987 and 1988.

Eastwood's politics and interests

Clint Eastwood is not one of those celebrities who likes to keep their personal opinions separate from the art they produce. He is a public figure and has even held a political office – he was mayor of the town of Carmel in California for two years. His interests in jazz music, military history and libertarian politics have played a large role in his work as a filmmaker.

Eastwood practices transcendental meditation and plays golf. He is an experienced pilot and is licensed to fly helicopters.

Clint Eastwood has been a passionate fan of jazz music for his entire life. He made the film biography *Bird* about the jazz saxophonist Charlie Parker in 1989, and the Secret Service agent he played in *In the Line of Fire* (1993) was also a jazz pianist. He has composed music for many of his films, including the title song for *Gran Torino*.

Clint Eastwood is a Libertarian. The Libertarian party was founded in Colorado in 1971. The basic beliefs of Libertarians are civil rights, freedom for capitalism, removing the welfare state and not getting mixed up in other countries' affairs. Eastwood has long spoken out against political correctness. He has been opposed to America's wars throughout his life, from the Korean (1950–1953) and Vietnam Wars (1964–1975) through to the Iraq War (2003–2011).

Eastwood believes, like most libertarians, in individualism and individual freedom. He has supported both Democrats and Republicans in the USA, depending on their individual policies on specific issues. He is pro-choice in the abortion debate and is a supporter of equal rights for women and for gay marriage. He is in favor of gun control and has said that he thinks that all privately owned guns should be officially registered. He has said that he doesn't see why any citizen should want or be allowed to own military-grade assault weapons.

Eastwood was opposed to the politics of President Barack Obama and said that he might be supporting Donald Trump in the 2016 elections, although he refused to say for certain.

Eastwood and "tough guys"

As an actor and a filmmaker, Clint Eastwood has consistently demonstrated throughout his career that one of the qualities he most respects and values is toughness. The characters he plays and the stories he tells are always, at some level, about the need to be tough in the face of adversity. His vision of toughness is not limited to being a literal tough guy: his film *Million Dollar Baby*, for example, is about a woman, and the character of Sue Lor in *Gran Torino* is one of the toughest in the film. Toughness does not mean being violent and being able to beat people up. It has a lot more to do with a very old–fashioned idea, a quality which Americans used to call "grit".

The idea of toughness has changed through his career. Beginning with the standard cowboy or gunslinger in his early Westerns, it has developed through the ambiguous Man With no Name and the ultra-violent Harry Callahan, while with his final Western *Unforgiven* he began to examine what being strong, brave and heroic in the face of adversity means when you get older and become more mature.

This development throughout his long career leads directly to the character of Walt Kowalski in *Gran Torino*. There are echoes of the anger and vigilantism of Harry Callahan, the grim misanthropy of the Man With no Name, and the older, wiser maturity of William Munny in *Unforgiven*. The decisions he makes at the end of the film show the growth and maturity of Eastwood's "tough guy" characters: he sacrifices himself to stop violence and does everything he can to stop Thao from heading down the path to violence and vengeance. Toughness has become separated from violence and vengeance and is more closely associated with strength of character, courage and compassion for other people in conflict situations.

Reception

The film was mostly positively received by critics and was commercially very successful. It remains one of the most respected and popular films in Eastwood's career. Negative reactions to the film by film critics tended to focus on questions of race, specifically the "white savior" issue (see below for more on this).

Box office

The term "box office" is used to refer to how much money a film has made in ticket sales for cinemas. Later, the additional sales of DVDs/ Blu-Rays or money made by licencing the film for use on television or streaming services adds to the amount of money a film can earn around the world.

Many studios focus on the opening weekend ticket sales in the USA for an indicator of how successful a film is going to be. In recent years, though, this approach has become less relevant. Other global markets are becoming more and more important, in particular China with its huge and growing middle-class population. What is popular in the USA may not work in China, and vice versa – the film adaptation of the online computer game *World of Warcraft* (2016), for example, flopped horribly in the USA and would have been a financial disaster for the studio which produced it, but it was a massive surprise hit in China, which eventually made it a commercial success

The success of a film is (to simplify things) a plus/minus sum with how much money it cost to make balanced against how much money it earns once it has been released. One factor which can influence whether a film is viewed as a success or a failure is the speed with which the film makes its money: some films are so-called slow burners, meaning they don't do well at the box office, but over time they develop a good reputation and become popular for a long time afterwards, earning back their money and cultivating a powerful and lasting reaction. Some examples include *Blade Runner* (1982), which made less money at the box office than it cost to make, but has since then become accepted as one of the greatest and most influential science fiction films of all, or *Fight Club* (1999), based on Chuck Palahniuk's novel and starring Brad Pitt, which made less than half its $63 million budget at the box office but became a cult hit and went on to make more than $100 million on video/DVD and remains very popular to this day.

Clint Eastwood has had his ups and downs at the box office. Some of his personal favorite projects, like the jazz biography film *Bird* (1988), were failures – the budget was around $14 million, and the film earned a little over $2 million at the box office, and has still not, years later, made enough money to have paid for itself. *Gran Torino* on the other hand was one of his biggest commercial successes.

The website BoxOfficeMojo.com is a reliable and widely-referenced resource for the commercial history of cinema around the world. It catalogues and analyses the financial performance of films in great detail. The statistics it lists for *Gran Torino* include ("gross" means the total amount of money earned):

Production budget:	$33 million
Total lifetime domestic (US) gross:	$148, 095, 302
Total lifetime worldwide gross	$121, 862, 926

On its wide opening weekend (its release to cinemas nationwide, across the USA) the film earned over $29 million: this means that it almost made its budget (how much it cost to produce) on the first weekend it was in cinemas. It was ranked #1 that weekend, meaning it was the most popular and successful film in the country. *Gran Torino* was in cinemas for a total of 189 days or 27 weeks, which is quite a long time for any film.

Looking at Clint Eastwood as an individual on the same website, we can see that his most commercially successful film to date as a director has been *American Sniper* (2014), with over $350 million earned worldwide. *Gran Torino* is his second most successful film. His two other major critical successes, the films for which he has received the most respect and praise, are *Unforgiven* (#4, $101 million) and *Million Dollar Baby* (#5, $100 million).

Ranked according to his films as an actor, his #1 most successful film is *Gran Torino*, followed by *In the Line of Fire* (1993).

In total, Clint Eastwood's films (including all films he has been involved with as actor and/or director) have made over $ 1.8 billion.

Critical reception

An aggregate website is a website which collects data and information from other sources and compiles it to produce both general (using mathematical averages) and detailed (the individual source data) information on a particular subject. The website rottentomatoes.com is one of the internet's oldest and most popular review aggregate sites: it gathers reviews of films (and TV shows, computer games, and other media) to give an at-a-glance average score to reflect the overall impression a film has made on reviewers, expressed as a percentage. The website also allows you to look at the individual reviews which were used to create the average score. Metacritic.com is another aggregate review site, more focussed on professional reviewers, and is also a very good source for finding overall reactions, as well as specific contemporary reviews of films and other media.

On rottentomatoes.com *Gran Torino* currently has an 80% rating. This is very high. It is based on 229 original reviews by professional critics, which have given the film an average score of 7.1/10. The film's rating is also affected by non-professional reactions from fans and normal cinemagoers (called the "audience score"). In this group the film has a 90 % positive rating.

The review by Geoff Andrew in the UK culture magazine *Time Out* described the film as a "comedy-drama" and says it is "actually a rather wise, insightful exploration of family and friendship, violence and vengeance"[1]. The film's focus is described as being "the encounter between Walt – a politically incorrect old bigot scarred by war – and today's multicultural society".

Richard Roeper[2] described the film as "a perfect, career-crowning performance for the macho icon […] a brilliant and challenging commentary on a lot of earlier Clint Eastwood roles". He also notes that

---

1 Time Out, 17.02.2009; www.timeout.com/london/film/gran-torino

2 www.richardroeper.com/reviews/id/47 (Stand: 01.07.2018)

"Eastwood is much too savvy and has been through far too much to be interested in serving up a simple dish of revenge fantasies".

Most other positive reviews follow these main points: that the film is an intelligent and mature look at themes like violence and family, and that it is an important and powerful performance (as an actor) and accomplishment (as a director) for Clint Eastwood. Many reviewers highlighted how the film and the character of Walt seemed to represent Eastwood's reflections on the iconic characters throughout his long career, specifically the ultra-violent vigilante Harry Callahan and the grim and misanthropic Man With no Name. Reviewers also praised the economic, efficient and unpretentious style of the film: Eastwood's unhurried direction and the film's script, which avoided being too sentimental and included a good amount of humor.

Awards

The film won the following awards:

American Film Institute: One of the Ten Best Films of 2008
National Board of Review: Best Actor (Clint Eastwood)
César Awards (Paris): Best Foreign Film

Gran Torino was nominated for several other awards, including a Golden Globe Award for Best Original Song and the Critics' Choice Award for Best Actor.

The film was not nominated for any Academy Awards (Oscars), which many people found surprising.

Negative reactions

Some reviewers thought that the film was too unsubtle in the way it handled its themes, or that it was too sentimental about old age and sacrifice. Some reviewers found Eastwood's performance to be too cliché, and some people reacted badly to the film's representation of Hmong-Americans.

One specific criticism of the film (cf.below) is the complaint, made by several reviewers, that it is an example of a "white savior narrative". It is one of the films that is always included in discussions of this issue.

The white savior narrative

Whereas Eastwood manages to tell a new kind of vigilante story in *Gran Torino* in which the vigilante manages to cleanse and save himself and others, the fact that he is a *white* savior can be seen as being more problematic. This is a complicated issue.

"White saviors" are white characters in films who save non-white characters from whatever trouble they may be in. White savior narratives also often include the idea that the white character uses the non-white culture to learn something new about him or herself.

This is an issue which has become more important in recent years as more and more films (and books, music, et cetera) have begun to deal with the reality of increasingly diverse societies. It has also become more common and widespread to question accepted versions of history which presented white Europeans as a force for freedom and civilization, bringing free trade, Christianity and good manners to all the dark corners of the world.

As societies become ethnically and culturally more diverse, the fact that almost all heroes/protagonists in mainstream films are white becomes harder to defend and explain. The problem is that critics see white savior films as showing non-white people who are not able to defend or save themselves: and also that it allows white characters to be presented as saviors, rather than representatives of a historically dominant culture which has enslaved, conquered and completely transformed non-white cultures all around the world.

Another major problem which critics of white savior narratives highlight is that these stories tend to portray white people as having some natural qualities, like courage, wisdom, goodness and above all leadership, which other races don't naturally possess.

A structural feature of white savior narratives is that they tend by definition to portray white characters as being active and non-white characters as being passive: the white guy is *saving* a black person who needs *to be saved*.

"White savior narrative" is an aggressive and argumentative label: it is not a genre. You can call *Gran Torino* a vigilante film because that's what the story is about – someone takes the law into their own hands. There's no room for argument there. To say that a film is a white savior narrative, however, means starting an argument about whether this is true or not.

Why *Gran Torino* is not a good example of a white savior narrative

The questions are: why are only white people capable of being heroes and saving others? Why can't/don't/won't the non-white characters save themselves? Applied to *Gran Torino* specifically, why do Sue and Thao need old white Walt to save them? What is it about Walt that makes him a savior?

We already see that Sue is a tough and self-confident young woman, capable of standing up for herself and her brother and completely unafraid of aggressive young men. Thao may lack a positive older male role model in his life and he may be an insecure and introverted young man, but he is also an integrated American teenager. When he is pressed too far by the gangsters (when they rape his sister) he wants to take action. He wants to rush out and take revenge. Neither of these characters is passive.

When thinking about *Gran Torino* and the accusation that it is a patronizing white savior narrative, we should remember that the violence is largely Walt's fault. He is indirectly to blame for the escalation of violence and the rape of Sue – without his actions (beating up Smokie) things would have been different. Nothing we know about this misanthropic old racist makes him a suitable example of white people being better or nobler than any other ethnicity.

Another factor to remember is Walt's age. The story does not *need* race to be an issue in order to function: the conflict could be between any fatherless teenage boy and a local gang trying to force him to join. What motivates the story is not a white American-Hmong division, but the division between a lonely old man and a directionless young boy. Walt does not try to teach Thao how to be white: he tries to teach him how to be a man.

▶ **Points to remember:**

- White savior films are historically insensitive and do not pay enough attention to the diverse nature of society.
- These films are told from a white perspective for a white audience, non-white identities are secondary in every way.
- They portray white characters as active and non-white characters as passive.
- They portray non-white cultures as being useful tools or environments allowing white people to learn more about themselves

Synopses

Scene by scene summaries and commentary

Time	Scene
00:00:00–00:09:15	**The funeral and the wake** Credits, soft music, and a funeral. Friends and relatives are paying their last respects to Dorothy Kowalski as her widower Walt looks on stonily. He is angry at the disrespectful appearance and behavior of his grandchildren. The young priest Father Janovich speaks about death. Walt is visibly annoyed by the young priest's comments on life and death. Afterwards at Walt's home the family is holding a wake: there is a lot of food and the grandchildren are digging around in Walt's things, looking at old photos of Walt in his time in the army during the Korean War. They also find a medal. Mitch tells his daughter Ashley to help her grandfather set up more chairs for the guests but he refuses her help. Walt takes his dog outside for a walk and sees Hmong women entering the house next door with food. When he returns, he finds Ashley smoking in the garage. She admires his Gran Torino and asks him what he plans on doing with it when he dies. She asks about other furniture he has: she doesn't realize at all how offended and angry he is. The doorbell rings and when Walt answers he see a young Hmong boy (Thao), who asks him if he can borrow jumper cables to help get his uncle's car started. Walt dismisses him rudely. He is then confronted by the priest, who calls him Walt ("Mr. Kowalski. That's my name.") and tells him Dorothy asked him to look after Walt and take his confession. Walt rejects him rudely. As the guests are leaving more and more Hmong are arriving next door. Walt sees a man beheading a live chicken and says they're barbarians.

▶	**Points to remember:** • Walt and his family are introduced in the opening scenes. • We learn a lot here about Walt's personality (his rudeness, coldness and racism) and his history (married to Dorothy; fought in the Korean War; worked at the Ford factory). • We are also introduced to three of the major stories the film will follow: a) Walt's estrangement from his own family b) the young priest's promise to take his confession c) his relationship with his Hmong neighbors.
00:09:15– 00:12:05	**The Hmong community, and Father Janovich visits Walt** The Hmong gathering Walt has noticed next door is to celebrate the birth of a child. There is a traditional service to bless the child and a lot of food for all the family members gathered there. Thao has been told by his sister Sue to do the washing up. The grandmother complains about Walt in her own language when she sees him cleaning up his front lawn. They have a brief spitting competition, which she wins. Father Janovich comes to visit Walt again and confronts him: Walt is very blunt in expressing his contempt for the young priest.
00:12:05– 00:17:20	**Gangsters** Thao is walking home when a group of young Latino men start racially and sexually harassing him. Thao's cousin Fong (Spider) and his friends are also driving around and see what is happening: they drive over to scare off the Latino gangsters. The gangs start shouting at each other and displaying their guns. The Latinos drive off. Fong and his friends bully Thao into getting into their car. They want him to get involved with their gang.

	Later on Fong and his friends drive past the Lors' home, where they again begin bullying Thao into joining them. Smokie tells Thao that he used to get bullied, too, until he joined a Hmong gang. Thao asks what he would have to do: they want him to steal Walt's car, the Gran Torino. ▶ **Points to remember:** • We meet Sue for the first time in the second scene with the Hmong gangsters. She is reading while Thao is working in the garden. • We are introduced to the Hmong gang, who bring about the turning point in the film.
00:17:20–00:22:00	**Walt at the bar, Father Janovich again: the attempted burglary** Walt is telling racist jokes at the bar with his friends. Father Janovich arrives and the two sit down to talk. Walt challenges Father J on his understanding of life and death. He talks about his experiences killing enemy soldiers during the Korean War. Father J challenges Walt on his fixation on death rather than life. That night Walt surprises Thao trying to steal the car. Thao runs away and Walt slips and falls. The next day Mitch calls while Walt is reinforcing his garage security. They have an awkward conversation and Walt hangs up on him. ▶ **Points to remember:** • Walt's relationships with the main characters, and the pattern of how all three try and get something from him in different ways: a) The priest works to get closer to Walt, in order to get his confession. He is willing to confront him about it. b) Thao tries but fails to steal his car, c) Mitch wants tickets to a sporting event but can't ask honestly for them, which indicates the terrible relationship he has with his father.

00:22:00– 00:27:10	**The Gran Torino: showdown with the gangsters on the front lawn** Walt is lovingly caring for his car. Then he and the dog sit on the porch and enjoy looking at the car. He drinks a few beers and goes to bed. That night, the Hmong gangsters return and try to take Thao with them. A huge fight follows and Walt breaks it up, threatening the gangsters with his gun. They leave. Sue thanks him and he tells her to get off his lawn. The next morning Walt is surprised to find the members of the Hmong community bringing him gifts of food and flowers. When he asks Sue why, she says that they are thanking him for having saved Thao. Thao apologizes to Walt for having tried to steal his car: Walt warns him to never again step on his property. ▶ **Points to remember:** • The showdown with the Hmong gangsters changes the dynamic between Walt and his neighbors. • We see a new, terrifying side to this grumpy old man, but also a first glimpse of Walt's moral values. He's a racist and a misanthrope, but he doesn't tolerate violence against the weak. That's an important message for the story which follows.
00:27:10– 00:30:00	**Father Janovich again and Martin the barber** Father J complains to Walt because he didn't call the police. He then urges him to confess, saying that he has been thinking about what Walt said about the horrors and violence of war, and how it would be good for him to unburden himself through the act of confession. Walt is impressed by the young priest's persistence but still refuses to confess. Later, Walt is at the barber's where he and Martin trade insults and racist slurs, enjoying each other's company.

▶	**Points to remember:** • We see further evidence of the darkness inside Walt. He suggests that he has done bad things without being ordered to. • Walt continues to express his contempt for the church, religion and faith. • Walt has a grudging respect for the priest's effort to do what he has promised he would do. • These two scenes contrast Walt's relationships: he and Martin are evidently on friendly terms but on a superficial level. The priest, who is attempting to get deeper into Walt's soul in order to help him, meets with forceful resistance from the old man, who doesn't *want* to change.
00:30:00–00:36:50	**Sue and her boyfriend harassed by African-Americans: Walt drives Sue home** Walking with her boyfriend, Sue is harassed by three young African-American men. The harassment is explicitly sexual and she confronts and mocks them for their racist stereotypes and the stereotypical way in which they behave. The situation becomes more threatening, and her boyfriend, who is white and obviously frightened by the black men, is no help. Walt is out driving in his pick-up truck and he sees the white boy being attacked and Sue being harassed. He watches Sue confronting the young men before driving over. The black men try to scare him off. Walt mimes pulling a gun and tells Sue to get in the truck: when the men still hold her, he suddenly pulls out a real gun. Sue gets in the truck. Driving home, Walt tells her off for having been in such a bad part of town ("I thought you Asian girls were supposed to be smart") and complains about her "goofball" boyfriend. Sue explains to him who the Hmong people are. They talk about Thao and Sue tells Walt about the difficulties Hmong boys have fitting in to American society, while the girls tend to do well.

▶	**Points to remember:** • In these scenes we get to know Sue a little better. She was unafraid in her confrontations with Walt and with the Hmong gang. Now we see her fearless confrontation with three very intimidating young men who are bigger than her and are threatening to rape her.
00:36:50– 00:40:20	**Horoscope, Thao helps the neighbor, Walt's birthday** Walt reads a horoscope from the newspaper about choices in life and second chances: he is pleasantly surprised to see Thao help an elderly neighbor. Mitch and Karen give Walt birthday presents. They try to persuade him to move out of his house and live in an assisted-living community for the elderly. Walt throws them out of his house in fury.
▶	**Points to remember:** • There is a comparison between the relationships Walt has with Sue and his son Mitch. He tells Sue that she's OK: they like and respect one another. Mitch seems to not understand his father at all: he only sees an old man and thinks that Walt is weak, lonely, and unable to look after himself. • The film offers different examples of how younger people treat the elderly Walt: the positive example of Sue, who treats him like a real person, and Mitch and Karen, who patronize him and treat him like a problem that has to be solved.
00:40:20– 00:51:30	**Walt at the Lor house; the shaman, food, Hmong customs, Thao and Youa** Sue invites Walt to a barbecue at her house and wishes him happy birthday. In the Lor house Walt learns more about Hmong customs, enjoys the food and has an encounter with the Lor family shaman. The shaman tells him he is not respected, that his food has no flavor, that he made a mistake in his life with which he is not satis-

	fied; that he has no happiness in his life, and that he is not at peace. Walt is upset by what the shaman says. He has a coughing fit, spitting up blood. He enjoys being fed by the older women in the family before Sue takes him to another part of the house to meet the younger Hmong. Walt notices that one of the girls (Youa) appears to have a crush on Thao. Walt and Youa talk. After she leaves (followed by the other boys there) Walt starts harassing Thao for not having taken his chance with a girl who obviously likes him.
▶	**Points to remember:** • The shaman's reading of Walt disturbs and upsets him. He reacts to it as if he feels the truth of it: and the camera shows us how Walt walks away from the shaman. Contrast his response to the way he dismisses the horoscope in the newspaper in the previous scene. • Walt looks at the contented, happy Hmong people spending time together, enjoying their sense of being together, of belonging. He misses this. • We also see a new and different side to Walt when he talks to Youa: he is more relaxed and funny, and he seems to feel more comfortable here amongst the Hmong than we have seen him so far during the film.
00:51:30-00:58:50	**Walt and Thao** The Hmong continue to bring Walt flowers and food, but he is happy to accept them now. Walt finds the Lor family on his doorstep: Sue explains that Thao has come to make amends for having tried to steal his car. Walt doesn't want to accept but Sue and her mother force him to. The next morning Thao surprises Walt by actually turning up. Walt eventually decides to have Thao clean up and renovate a run-down house on the other side of the street. Walt observes Thao, who is working very hard. Other Hmong come to Walt to ask if Thao can do things for them to, because they have seen what a hard worker he is.

	On the morning of his last day working for Walt, Thao is disappointed when Walt tells him they're done and he doesn't need to work for him anymore.
►	**Points to remember:** • The relationship between Walt and Thao grows from mutual dislike to mutual affection and trust. • Walt sees that Thao is a disciplined, responsible boy who is willing to work hard. • Thao is given, for the first time, a strong male role model who demands respect, and in return gives respect which has been earned. • Thao's eagerness to work provide an insight into how much Thao has already changed, and how Walt's use of hard work has made him feel better about himself.
00:58:50–01:01:10	**Walt at the doctor's, talking to Mitch** Walt is waiting to see his doctor. He is uncomfortable, looking at the non-white people around him, including the nurse in a headscarf and the Asian-American doctor who has replaced his old doctor, long retired. Later he calls his son Mitch to talk, and we see that he has received test results from the doctor.
►	**Points to remember:** • There is more of Walt's racism (his clear dislike of non-whites) • His health issues are fairly serious. • The telephone conversation shows that Walt's behavior has consequences. He tries to reach out to his son, who doesn't really want to talk to him.
01:01:10-01:08:00	**Gangster drive by; Walt and Thao begin to bond in various situations** The Hmong gangsters drive down the street, menacing Thao and Walt. Walt mimes pointing and firing a gun at them. He mutters to himself that Thao doesn't stand a chance against this kind of pressure.

Thao needs Walt's help fixing something in their kitchen. Walt decides to begin fixing other things in the Lor house. He shows Thao his tools and gives the boy a couple of basic things. He offers to lend the boy anything else he may need.
Walt coughs blood again and Thao is concerned. Walt then asks the boy what is going on with the Hmong gangsters. He is surprised when Thao tells him he was supposed to steal the Gran Torino as an initiation ceremony to join the gang.
Walt is struggling to get his old freezer out of the cellar: he has to ask Thao for help. Thao insists on carrying the heavy end of the fridge. Walt agrees to sell Thao the freezer for $25.
Thao is cleaning the Gran Torino in the yard. Sue and Walt are talking: she tells him how good he is for helping Thao and for being a positive role model. She compares Walt to their father (who is dead) and implies he is a better father figure. She also points out, against Walt's protests, that the old man actually likes Thao.

Points to remember:

- These are key scenes for the relationship between Thao and Walt.
- Thao is concerned by Walt's illness; Walt is concerned about Thao's problems with the Hmong gangsters.
- Walt turns to Thao for help to move his freezer out of the cellar – unusual for a man who never asks for help.
- Thao uses strong language to make Walt accept help. He sounds like a man, so Walt follows his advice.
- Thao cleans the Gran Torino in the yard as Walt and Sue watch.
- Sue explicitly identifies Walt as a father figure and as a role model for Thao.

01:08:00–01:10:30	**Career advice** Walt and Thao are talking while Thao is helping in Walt's garden. Walt talks about his career, working in the Ford factory, and he asks Thao what he wants to do with his life. Thao is unsure, and Walt suggests the boy get a job in construction to save money for college. ▶ **Points to remember:** • Walt and Thao talk like father and son, bringing together the themes of family, masculinity and belonging.
01:10:30–01:17:00	**"Man you up"** **Guy talk** Walt takes Thao to see Martin to learn "how guys talk". **Getting a job** Walt takes Thao to apply for a job working on a construction site run by his friend Kennedy ("you drunken Irish goon"). **Hardware** Walt buys Thao his first tools. When Thao says he can't pay for it, Walt tells him he'll pay, and Thao can pay him back out of his first paycheck. The scene ends with Thao thanking Walt and them shaking hands. ▶ **Points to remember:** • Thao is very sceptical after hearing Walt and Martin trade crude racial and homophobic insults. But he plays along, imitating the offensive language used by the two men. • **Guy talk:** this is comical scene about masculinity, showing how dumb stereotypical "guy talk" can be. • Walt teaching Thao how to get a job and buying him his first tools provide more depth to the father-son relationship. • The handshake at the end is a significant display of the respect and friendship between the two.

01:17:00– 01:21:00	**The Hmong gangsters** Thao is coming home from work when the Hmong gangsters ambush him. They beat him up, put out a cigarette on his face and steal or break his and Walt's tools. Later, when Walt sees him, Thao tries to tell Walt that it's all OK, but the old man seems worried and angry. Walt has found where the gangsters live and is parked outside their house watching them. He grabs one of the gang, beats him up and threatens him with a gun, telling him to stay away from Thao or things will get ugly.
01:21:00- 01:27:00 ▶	**The drive-by shooting and the rape** Walt returns home. It is raining. It looks like he is in pain after beating up the gangster. The next day he is barbecuing and having a good time with the Lors. Everyone is happy: Walt and Sue tease each other and Thao has asked Youa out on a date. Walt offers to lend Thao the Gran Torino. At night: Walt is watching TV when the Hmong gangsters drive by and suddenly start shooting into the Lors' house. Walt rushes over to find the Lors shocked but unhurt. But Sue is missing. Walt and the Lors can't find her, and he waits with them. A car pulls up and Sue returns. She has been beaten and raped. In a rage, Walt returns to his house and destroys his kitchen. He sits down in his chair in the dark and begins to focus his anger. **Points to remember:** • The weather plays a role: it is raining and dark and ominous when Walt arrives home – a signal that trouble is coming. Walt's actions have set something dangerous in motion. • The drive-by shooting is a warning: the rape of the Sue by the Hmong gangsters is the real crisis. This is the tipping point in the narrative

01:27:00- 01:29:00	**Father Janovich** The priest comes to visit Walt, who is still sitting in the dark. He has been looking at old photos of him with his wife. They talk, and Walt shows him more respect than he has so far. They have a beer and talk about what Walt should do to respond to the violence. Walt is thinking hard about what he should do. **Points to remember:** • This scene finishes the journey Walt and Father Janovich have been on together. The old man offers the priest respect, tells him to call him Walt, and asks him for advice. The priest has also changed in his attitude: he knows that Walt can't be reached with simple clichés, and that the old man wants more truth, even if that is only admitting "I don't know". • This scene is an example of narrative tension. Nothing "happens" yet: but all the talk about vengeance implies that a showdown is approaching. We don't know what is about to happen: Walt doesn't either. He is considering his options. We are all kept in suspense.
01:29:00– 01:39:20	**Walt prepares for the end** Thao comes to Walt's house the next morning demanding action. Walt is thinking. Thao wants to kill the gangsters. Walt tells him that they have to plan their revenge carefully: he says Thao should go home and return that afternoon, and "what needs to be done will be done". Walt mows his lawn, takes a bath, has a haircut and shave at Martin's, has a fitted suit done at a tailor's, and then visits Father Janovich in the church to make his confession. Thao comes back that afternoon to find Walt cleaning his guns. Walt gives Thao his Silver Star (a military decoration for courage in combat). He then shuts the boy

	in the cellar. He tells Thao that he is haunted by the memory of a young Korean soldier he had killed: he wants to save Thao from making a mistake and destroying his life with violent vengeance. Walt takes his dog next door and gives her to the Lor grandmother. He then calls Sue to tell her that Thao is locked in his house. As he had promised, Father Janovich is waiting outside the Hmong gang house with the police, who say nothing is happening, and leave. He wants to stay but the police force him to come with them. Sue finds Thao and lets him out. ► **Points to remember:** • Walt makes sure there are no loose ends in his life. He is keeping promises, putting his affairs in order, and doing all he can to make sure those close to him will be OK. • It is obvious that Walt is preparing to die: but we still don't know what his plan is.
01:39:20– 01:43:00	**The end** Night: Walt is outside the Hmong gang house. They see him from inside and come out. Walt starts to provoke them: they are surprised he came and not Thao, who they wanted. Neighbors in the street hear the voices and come out to watch what is happening. Walt reaches into his pocket for a cigarette, and the gangsters pull their guns. He mimes pointing and shooting a gun at them. Walt reaches into his coat, saying the Hail Mary prayer, and the gangsters panic and shoot him. All the neighbors gathered to watch see them gun down an unarmed old man with a cigarette lighter. The police arrest the gangsters: Thao and Sue arrive in the Gran Torino. Thao desperately tries to get past the police, and one Hmong policeman tells him what happened. Father Janovich is also there. The camera fades out on the silver star medal pinned to Thao's t-shirt.

01:43:00	**The funeral and the will**
	The Lors, in traditional Hmong costumes, go to Walt's funeral. Father Janovich speaks fondly of Walt. Thao and Mitch are both obviously heartbroken by Walt's death. Afterwards, Walt's will is read in a lawyer's office. The final item is the Gran Torino: Ashley is smiling and expects to get it, but Walt has left it to Thao. The film closes with music as we watch Thao and Daisy in the Gran Torino, driving along the shoreline of Lake Michigan.
▶	**Points to remember:** • There is a symmetry between the opening (Dorothy's funeral) and the end (Walt's funeral). • The final scene moves beyond the closed narrative system of symmetry and shows us the future: Thao has with Walt's help become a man. Thao in the Gran Torino is moving into the future, with more hope and more strength than he could have imagined at the beginning of the film.

Characters

The Kowalski family

Walter "Walt" Kowalski

Walt is the central character in the film. He is an elderly Polish-American man who worked for many years in the Ford car factory in Detroit. He fought in the Korean War (1950–1953). For background information on Detroit and the Korean War see Setting and context, p. 102. During the war he killed a young Korean soldier who had been trying to surrender to him, and this event haunts him. His wife Dorothy has just died and he now lives alone with his dog Daisy in his old neighborhood, surrounded by Asian immigrants. He has two sons, the elder of whom has two children.

Walt becomes involved with his Hmong neighbors after Thao tries to steal his car. He later drives the gangsters away, defending the Lor family, and in doing so becomes more involved with the family and their feud with the gang. He enjoys spending time with the Hmong community and takes on the role of a father figure for Thao, teaching the boy how to be a man. When he beats up one of the Hmong gangsters in response to their attack on Thao, Walt unintentionally escalates the feud. The gang shoot up the Lor house in a drive-by and kidnap and rape Sue. To save Thao from destroying his own life by trying to kill the gangsters in revenge, Walt tricks the gangsters into shooting him in front of witnesses, sacrificing himself to end the cycle of violence and to give Thao the chance to live a free life.

Misanthrope (*noun*), misanthropy (*noun*), misanthropic (*adjective*) – from the Greek, misos "hatred" + anthropos "human"

This is a key word for describing and interpreting Walt Kowalski. A misanthrope is a person who hates and avoids other people, which is the impression Walt gives of himself when we first meet him. He seems to hate everyone, even his own family. He seizes on the opportunity to take his dog Daisy out for a walk just so that he can get away from the people in his house. He uses offensive and rude language and behavior to drive people away from him.

His misanthropy comes in part from his intolerance of fools and bad behavior (see how he reacts to his grandchildren), but also his contempt for anything he sees as being weak. He is also, we learn much later in the film, tortured by guilt for having killed a boy in the Korean War. This guilt and the anger it feeds in him contribute a lot to his misanthropic behavior.
This (dominant) aspect of Walt's character becomes softer as the film progresses thanks to his friendship with Sue and Thao Lor. He becomes gentler, more relaxed and friendlier.

Walt is not an easy man to like. He is unfriendly to everyone, rude to people who try to talk to him, and he is a racist. He evidently dislikes his own children and grandchildren; he treats the young priest with contempt; he insults his Hmong neighbors. He seems to be angry all the time. When we get to know him early in the film, the only things he seems to show any affection for are his dog Daisy and his car, the Gran Torino. He is so misanthropic that it is almost comic.

To balance this negative first impression, we should remember that Walt is an old man whose beloved wife has just died, and that he is watching the world he knew changing and vanishing before his eyes. He finds it very hard to let go of the past (represented by the car and his military keepsakes, like guns and medals). He is also very ill and possibly dying, which he hides from everyone around him.

This is the starting point for our understanding of Walt as a character. *Gran Torino* is very much about how his friendship with Sue and Thao Lor changes him, so the development of Walt's character through the film starts when he first begins to interact with the Lor family.

The evolution of Walt: his friendship with Sue and Thao

The softening between Walt and the Hmong neighbors really begins when he rescues Sue from being harassed by a group of young men (00:30:00). He has already protected Thao and Sue by driving the gangsters away with his rifle (00:24:00), but he has rejected their attempts to show their gratitude. It is only once he and Sue are sitting in the car together talking that he begins to open up. He watched how she reacted when she was being harassed and was obviously impressed by her toughness and ability to fight back. He likes the fact that she is not offended by his crude racism, and is even able to hit back, creating a similar kind of comic-offensive banter as he has with his barber, Martin. He tells her "you're alright" (00:36:25): he clearly enjoys talking to her.

He grows closer to Thao after Sue and her mother force him to take Thao on so that the latter can atone for having tried to steal Walt's car. This process is at the heart of the film, thematically and in the narrative. Sue encourages Walt to see himself as a father figure to the shy and aimless boy, and Walt accepts the role. He sets out to make a man of Thao.

Walt and Mitch

This process of surrogate father-son bonding between Walt and Thao runs parallel to the decay of Walt's relationship with his own family, in particular his son Mitch. This decay is presented in three key scenes – two telephone conversations and a visit on Walt's birthday.

– Mitch calls Walt (00:21:00)

Essentially, Mitch wants to get some free tickets for a sporting event and he knows his dad knows a guy. But he tries to hide this, even when Walt directly asks him "what do you want?" This conversation shows the father and son unable to communicate: Mitch is not honest with his father, and Walt rejects Mitch. He does not respect his son and he does not want to waste time talking to him.

– The visit (00:38:36)

Mitch and Karen Kowalski visit Walt on his birthday to give him presents, and to persuade him to move out of the house into an assisted living facility for the elderly. The gifts are, for a man like Walt, deeply insulting – a stick to pick up objects so he doesn't have to get up, and a telephone with huge buttons for old people who cannot see properly any more and have poor hand-eye coordination. They suggest weakness and a lack of self-sufficiency, they tell him that Karen and Mitch think he is no longer able to look after himself and be an independent man. Walt erupts like a volcano, throwing them out of his house, and we see them taking their presents with them. This scene is both comic and informative. We learn here that Mitch simply does not know or understand his father, and that Walt values his independence and self-sufficiency very highly.

– Walt calls Mitch (00:59:48)

This scene mirrors the earlier phone call. Walt has just received bad news about his health. He knows he is dying. He calls his son because he is scared and lonely: but the years of coldness and rejection have had an effect, and Mitch does not like talking to his father either. He does not understand why his father would call him up just to chat, and it is only after they hang up and the camera lingers on Mitch's face that we can see that maybe he senses something is wrong – this is obviously unusual behavior for his notoriously misanthropic father. But the bond between father and son is so damaged and weak by this point that Mitch does nothing. The next time we see Mitch is at his father's funeral.

Walt's relationship with Mitch is subtly held up against his evolving bond with Thao throughout the film, and this link is seen during Walt's funeral, when the two characters, Walt's real son and his surrogate son, look at each other across the church, both heartbroken at the loss of the old man. We can interpret into this sad scene that it is Thao who will come away with more of Walt's love and more of his presence in his life: Walt and Mitch's relationship, as he confesses to Father Janovich, has been broken for a long time.

Walt's interactions with other characters

Walt's interactions with the following characters are significant as they help us understand his character and how he changes and evolves during the film.

- Sue is the first person we see in the film who is able to have a real relationship with Walt. She is grateful to him for having driven off the gang and saved her from being harassed, and he respects her toughness and strength. Through her, Walt gets to know the Hmong and discovers a second family towards the end of his life. His friendship with Sue allows him to relax, to become friendlier, funnier and more tolerant.

- Thao becomes a surrogate son for Walt. He calls him his friend, and after a difficult start (Thao tries to steal Walt's car, Walt threatens him with a gun) they become very close. Walt puts a lot of time and energy and care into helping Thao become a man. He helps him find himself and his place in the world. At the end, Walt sacrifices himself so that Thao can be free (from the threat of the Hmong gang).
- Father Janovich represents a number of things in the film, with the most important being that he is keeping a promise to Walt's dead wife Dorothy, and so in a way he represents her. While Walt dismisses the inexperienced young priest, the Church and religion in general, he still finds it difficult to ignore or reject Father Janovich completely. He respects the priest's persistence, and he is forced to think about what he says about life and death. The two men challenge each other's attitudes, and Walt has a profound influence on how the young priest thinks about life and death.
- Youa does not play a big role in the story, but she brings out another side of Walt's character that we have not seen before. He seems to respond very well to women: he feels at ease with the older Hmong women who feed him, and both Sue and Youa find it easy to engage him in conversation, in particular when compared with Father Janovich or Thao. Youa is an example of how Walt's *actual* response to people may differ from his theatrical, racist misanthropy.

Points to remember:

- Walt is a working-class military veteran of the Korean War and a widower.
- He is racist and intolerant of any sign of foolishness or stupidity. He has no problem showing this, too.
- During his military service in the Korean War, Walt killed a young Korean soldier who had been trying to surrender, and this has haunted him for his entire life.
- Walt is alienated from his family. As he confesses to the priest, he never learned how to talk to his sons, and he regrets this.
- He has no respect for the Catholic Church or for religion. He does however have a strong moral code.

- Walt's friendship with Sue and Thao Lor suggest that his racist views are less important to him than his enjoyment of the Hmong community and his friendship with the two young people.
- When Walt becomes involved in the feud between the Hmong gangsters and the Lor family, he makes things worse despite only trying to help.
- Walt's sacrifice is the only way he can find to end the cycle of violence which has begun.

Key scenes:

As he is the main character, the film is full of important scenes and significant quotations to help us describe and analyze the character of Walt Kowalski. Here are a few key examples.

00:24:00 Walt's menacing threat of violence drives the Hmong gangsters off. In this scene we catch a sight of the man who killed during the war. He is a cold, terrifying presence. The gangsters are intimidated and run away. Despite his age, Walt is a very threatening and dangerous figure, and we identify him with guns, threats, and the ice-cold calm of a trained killer. This impression is important, in particular in relation to the way Walt sacrifices himself at the end of the film.

00:38:00 Walt sees Thao helping an elderly neighbor pick up her groceries. Despite his dislike of the boy he considers to be "slow" and who he caught trying to steal his car, Walt approves of Thao's behavior here, setting the scene for the relationship which will develop between the two. We see here, and from this point on, that Walt is able and willing to look past his negative first impression of the boy and give him a second chance – one example of the theme of people being given second chances in this story.

00:40:40 "We miss Mama, Daisy, don't we?" – Walt is lonely. He wouldn't show it to others, and he rejects his son's efforts to put him in an assisted living facility (in the scene immediately before this), but he admits to his dog that he misses his wife. He is alone and surrounded by strangers from a (for him) strange culture. This short scene comes between the frustrating encounter with his "real" family on his birthday and the surprisingly enjoyable afternoon he spends with his Hmong neighbors, where he is welcomed into a friendly and generous community. It is a significant moment in the film, helping to explain why he is so receptive to the generosity and hospitality of his Hmong neighbors.

00:49:50 "I've been called a lot of things, but never funny." In talking to Youa, however brief the conversation is, Walt learns something new about himself: that given the right people and the right context, he can be something he didn't know he was. One big topic in the film is the growth of Walt as a person, which is important because it is a development happening very late in the life of an elderly conservative. Walt's exposure to the new worlds of Sue and Thao – young, Hmong, immigrant – helps him to grow as an individual. He becomes more knowledgeable, more tolerant, his horizons are widened and he discovers a warmth and a goodness inside himself.

00:58:40 After being surprised and pleased at how well Thao can work, Walt seems to be about to congratulate the boy, or thank him, or in some way express something positive, but at the last second he stops himself. Walt is not quite ready yet to open himself up by showing warmth. The misanthropy which has defined him so far is breaking down: but it's not yet quite gone. He can't yet bring himself to show and affection or respect for the boy.

01:35:00 Walt tells Thao why he has locked him in the cellar: it is because he is haunted by the memory of a young Korean soldier he killed during the war, and he is unable to escape from this memory. This is the darkness inside Walt, which the Hmong shaman saw, and which Father Janovich also knows is there. But Walt only confesses to Thao. He wants to save Thao from the same fate, to stop him from doing something stupid (killing the Hmong gangsters who raped his sister) and having to live forever with their blood on his hands. If the development of Walt in the film can be interpreted as a gradual opening of a cold and distant man to the world around him, then this is the final part of him which has to open: he exposes the guilt and darkness within himself, the source of his anger and coldness.

Dorothy Kowalski

Walt's wife. She has recently died when the film begins: the opening scenes take place at her funeral and wake. While Dorothy doesn't appear in the film her presence is felt quite strongly. Four things are important when thinking about the character of Dorothy Kowalski.

Firstly, she was obviously the person who held the Kowalski family together. Walt has no patience with his sons or grandchildren, who he thinks are weak and spoiled.

Secondly, she was a devout Catholic and had made Father Janovich promise to take Walt's confession (see conversation between Father Janovich and Walt at the wake: 00:07:20). While Walt rejects Catholicism, Father Janovich and religion in general, this theme is important in the film and very important for an understanding of what happens at the end of the film and why. Dorothy's presence is very strong in this central aspect of *Gran Torino*.

Thirdly, it is clear from the way people talk about her – in particular the priest, Father Janovich – that Dorothy had acted as a kind of filter between Walt and the world around him, softening his misanthropy and making him behave in society. She was obviously the person who shielded Walt from the world – and vice versa. With her gone, he has no one to act as a buffer between his rough personality and the people around him. He feels lonely and isolated and is forced by circumstances to grow as a person: to become more open. He thinks that his own family is useless and he rejects them. His friendship with his Hmong neighbors at the end of his life tells us a lot about how his wife had organized their lives, and how he had evidently been isolated from many aspects of the world around him.

And finally, Dorothy is an interesting example of a rare kind of fictional character who is important *because* she is not there. She only exists as a negative space, as a kind of silhouette, and in the film we see Walt adapting to this absence and dealing with the space she used to inhabit in his life.

▶ Points to remember:

- Walt's dead wife was a devout Catholic and wanted him to make a confession. She made the priest promise to get Walt to confess.
- She was the person who held the family together.

Key scenes:

- The film begins with Dorothy's funeral: a lot of people have come to church to pay their respects. This tells us that she was well-loved.

Mitch Kowalski – older son

Karen Kowalski – Mitch's wife
Ashley Kowalski – Mitch and Karen's daughter
Josh Kowalski – Mitch and Karen's son

Mitch is the elder of Walt's two sons. He is married and has two children. He is a salesman, selling Japanese-made cars, much to Walt's disgust.

Walt disapproves of Mitch and his lifestyle and Mitch knows it. They have a difficult relationship, with Walt more or less openly expressing contempt for his son and grandchildren, and Mitch in turn trying to move his father into a nursing home. Karen dislikes Walt – she finds his cold, harsh manner very offensive and difficult to deal with. They also complain about Walt's racism.

The grandchildren are openly disrespectful and are portrayed in the film in quite a negative way: we see Josh making jokes during his grandmother's funeral (00:01:20) and Ashley telling Walt which of his possessions she wants when he dies, including his beloved car and some of his furniture (00:05:50). It is striking in this scene how completely unaware Ashley is of the effect her insensitivity is having on her grandfather: he is obviously angry and offended, but she doesn't notice this at all. We learn from this scene that she is self-obsessed and insensitive to the feelings of other people, and also that she is greedy and spoiled: she expects to get anything she wants. She is completely stunned when, during the reading of the will after Walt's death, she learns that she isn't going to inherit his Gran Torino (01:45:00).

Mitch is similar: when he calls his father (00:21:00) he claims it's just to see how he's doing, but what he actually wants is to get some tickets to a sporting event. Walt comments sarcastically about Karen having already taken Dorothy's jewelry, and Mitch, like his wife and daughter, exposes himself here as someone who is not interested in Walt except as a source of (material) things.

The tables are turned, however, in a later phone call. After Walt gets bad test results from the doctor he is scared and lonely and calls his son: Mitch tries to make the phone call as brief as possible. He doesn't enjoy Walt's company any more than his father enjoys his. After they hang up, though, Mitch's expression, which the camera stays on for a few seconds, is thoughtful and maybe even worried. It is unusual for his father to reach out to chat – maybe in this scene Mitch feels that something is wrong with his father.

Points to remember:

- Mitch is Walt's eldest son. They have a very bad relationship.
- Mitch works selling Japanese cars, which Walt sees as a betrayal of everything he did in his life and everything he holds dear.
- The grandchildren are portrayed in the film as disrespectful, spoiled and greedy.
- Walt confesses to Father Janovich that he never learned to talk to his sons, and we see this truth throughout the film.

Key scenes:

- (00:04:27) Ashley at the wake for her dead grandmother: "How much longer do we have to stay? This ghetto is a dead zone for my cell and I'm *bored*."
- (00:21:00 and 00:59:48) The two telephone conversations: Mitch calls because he wants tickets; Walt calls because he's scared about his health. On both occasions they talk past each other and refuse or are unable to connect.
- (01:09:00) Walt on Mitch: "I work in the Ford factory for 50 years, and he's out selling Japanese cars."
- (01:33:50) Walt to Father Janovich, during confession: "I was never very close to my two sons. I don't know 'em. I didn't know how."

The Hmong family

Sue Lor

Sue is a teenaged girl. She is the most outgoing member of the Lor family: she is confident, tough and not afraid to face up to challenges. She has a very positive and strong personality. She can stand up to young men who are trying to sexually harass her (00:30:00) as well as her sociopathic cousin and his gang (00:15:00). She is not offended or scared off by Walt's rude manner and blatant racism (she comments sarcastically on Walt's crude racist attitudes: "Wow, you're so enlightened!" 00:35:35) and earns his respect for being tough and direct.

As the feud between the gang and the Lor family escalates, Sue is abducted, beaten and raped by members of her cousin's gang. This is in response to Thao's resistance and Walt having beaten up one of the gang members.

Points to remember:

- Sue is a tough and intelligent young woman. She earns Walt's respect with her fearlessness, straightforward manner and refusal to take offence.
- She likes Walt and makes efforts to bring him into her family and community, apparently seeing how lonely he is, and also understanding that he is not a bad man, despite his misanthropic exterior.
- She is well-integrated into American society.
- She is targeted by the Hmong gangsters due to the fact that she is Thao's sister.

Key scenes:

- Sue first appears 15 minutes into the film, where she fights back against the gangsters when they start harassing Thao.
- (00:30:00) Sue and her boyfriend are harassed by young black men. While the boy is terrified and unable to respond, Sue fights back fiercely. Walt observes this and rescues her. It is a key scene for understanding why he takes an interest in her, and it is a clear display of her strength of character.

- (00:41:00) "I'm kidding, you moron!" Sue enjoys giving as good as she gets when Walt is acting ignorant and racist. He enjoys this back-and-forth banter, too.
- (00:46:00) "Come on, you glutton!": more of their teasing banter.
- (01:05:00) Sue and Walt talk while watching Thao clean the Gran Torino: the two have become close. Sue wishes that her father had been more like Walt, underlining the surrogate father role he has come to play for the two young people.

Thao Vang Lor

Thao is a teenaged boy who lives with his family next door to Walt. He is a quiet and introverted boy who, as his sister tells Walt, lacks a sense of direction. Thao is bullied by a gang into trying to steal Walt's car. Walt chases him off. The Lor family force Thao to work for Walt to make amends for what he did. Thao shows that he can work hard and is willing to face up to his responsibilities. Walt takes more of an interest in the boy and, influenced by Sue, takes more of a father-figure role. He sets out to help the boy become a man. Thao learns from Walt how to get a job, use tools and deal with other men. He becomes a more confident person. When his sister is raped by the Hmong gang, Thao wants to take revenge, but Walt stops him, thereby saving him from destroying his life by making a terrible mistake. At the end of the film Thao has been saved by Walt – from both the gang and his own aimlessness – and has inherited the Gran Torino. The film closes with Thao driving off into the distance.

Thao is shy and lacks direction, but he is by nature kind and helpful: Walt is pleasantly surprised when he sees Thao helping a neighbor when she drops her groceries (00:38:00). The first real conversation he has with Walt is at the barbecue (00:50:00), where the old man harasses him about girls. And then his mother and sister force him to offer to work for Walt to make amends for having tried to steal the car (00:52:00). Walt has low expectations – he still thinks the boy is slow and useless.

Walt and Thao begin to bond over work. Walt makes the boy work, sees that he's good at it, and respects him for it: and Thao in turn learns to respect himself and find some kind of focus. Being with Walt makes him more confident. He begins to assert himself more, he is less offended by Walt's rudeness and roughness, and as he becomes more capable he becomes stronger as a person. Walt is, as Sue points out, the father and role model Thao was missing. He is teaching the boy to be a man.

As a surrogate son, Thao becomes very important to Walt, who is alienated from his own sons. Thao likes and respects Walt and is heart-broken at his funeral. The end of the film, with Thao driving off in the Gran Torino, suggests that Walt has saved Thao in more ways than one. Not only by stopping him from being killed by the gang or ending up in jail for killing someone himself: Walt has also shown Thao how to confront the world with confidence and respect, to be strong and honest, and to value honest work. Thao has been given a second chance at life through his friendship with Walt and has been given the chance to have a future which, as Sue tells Walt (00:36:30), Hmong boys seldom have.

Points to remember:

- Having direction and knowing yourself. This is Thao's weakness, something he struggles with, and this is what Walt helps him with. It is not unusual for teenagers not to know exactly who they are and where they are heading in life, but Thao is very vulnerable to bad influences (the gang) and does not have a stable, strong male role model in his life.
- Thao is a kind young man with a good heart. He likes to work and wants to go to college to study.
- Thao becomes a surrogate son for Walt, who cannot deal with his own sons, and Walt becomes a surrogate father for Thao, whose real father is dead and was not a good father while he was alive.

Key scenes:

(00:19:50) Thao tries to steal the Gran Torino: Walt surprises him and threatens him with a rifle. Thao runs away.

(00:36:00) Sue talking to Walt about Thao: "Thao is actually really smart. He just doesn't know what direction to go in."

(00:38:00) Walt sees Thao run across the road to help an old lady who has dropped her groceries.

(00:50:00) Walt and Thao have their first conversation. This is mostly Walt insulting Thao for being a "pussy" and giving him advice on how to get girls.

(00:54:10) Walt: "What are you good at?" Thao: "I don't know." The boy is aimless, insecure, lacking in confidence and direction. He doesn't know how to talk to this difficult, stern old man. Working for Walt gives him direction.

(00:55:00) When Walt gets Thao to renovate and tidy up the old house across the street, things start to change. The boy works hard and does a good job. The music emphasizes the warmer feeling in the film as Walt watches with growing admiration and respect. Thao learns something about himself, too: that he enjoys working and doing something useful.

(00:57:55) At the end of this scene, Thao looks disappointed when Walt tells him they have finished the work. Thao enjoys working. This is a significant scene for understanding Thao as a character.

(01:01:00) Despite having learned that it was Thao's "last day" (00:58:30) working for Walt, we see him still working in Walt's garden when the Hmong gangsters drive down the street. He does not need to be working there any more, so we can assume that he is continuing to work because he wants to, and that Walt is letting him because he also enjoys spending time with the boy.

(01:05:35) "No, I'm here because *you* need help." Thao has become assertive. He knows he can help the old man: he is forcing Walt to acknowledge that he needs help. This scene sets them on a much more equal level, as Walt has to admit that he needs Thao's help.

(01:17:00) Walt and Thao shake hands in the hardware store. This is a significant moment, a gesture of friendship, equality and respect between the old man and the young man.

(01:23:00) Walt offers to lend Thao the Gran Torino so he can take Youa on a date. This is a big step, when we consider Thao's first encounter with Walt and his car.

(01:36:00) Walt locks Thao in the cellar to stop him from trying to avenge his sister by attacking the gangsters. Thao is furious at being kept locked up: he doesn't fully understand why Walt would do this. He still thinks Walt is going to attack the gangsters alone. Thao is furious and frustrated here.

Grandma Lor

The first-generation Hmong matriarch is an impressive presence. She comments rudely about Walt, and the two old people spend a lot of time sitting on their porches being suspicious of one another. At the end of the film, when he is preparing for the end, Walt gives her his dog Daisy to look after, knowing that she will take care of Daisy and probably enjoy the dog's company (01:37:25). Grandma Lor worries about her daughter, Vu Lor, whose husband has recently died, not having a husband and a man in the house. She doubts that Thao will ever be able to be a man because he lets his sister order him around.

The Hmong gang

The two main characters in the Hmong gang are:
- "Smokie", a fat young man with a shaved head, is aggressive and threatening. Walt beats him up (01:20:00) after the gangsters hurt Thao and steal his stuff.
- Fong ("Spider") is Thao's cousin. He tries to recruit Thao into their gang.

The Hmong gang represents the greatest threat in the film. They want Thao to join their gang, and the pressure they increasingly put on him leads to a backlash from Walt, which in turn leads to a cycle of violence. This is the sequence of events, briefly summarizing all scenes in which the gang appears:

1. They want Thao to join their gang after protecting him from being harassed by some Chicano gangsters (00:12:00).
2. They bully Thao into trying to steal the Gran Torino as an initiation ritual (00:15:00 – the attempted theft comes at 00:20:00).
3. When Thao refuses to come with them, they try to abduct him, leading to a brawl which Walt stops by threatening to shoot them (00:23:50).

4. The gang drives slowly past where Walt and Thao live, apparently intending to scare the boy. Walt menaces them with his mimed gun and Smokie gives him the middle finger (01:01:00).
5. They ambush Thao, beat him up, put out a cigarette on his face and steal and break his tools (01:17:00).
6. In response to this Walt finds out where they live and beats up Smokie, warning him to stay away from Thao (01:20:00).
7. They then do a drive-by shooting at the Lor house, then kidnap and rape Sue (01:23:00).
8. Walt tricks the gang into shooting him in front of witnesses (01:39:00). The police take them away, saying that they'll be going to jail for many years.

Other characters

Father Janovich

Father Janovich is an important character. The Polish-American Catholic priest is a young man (Walt says he's 27) who was close to Walt's dead wife, and who promised her that he would get Walt to come to church and make his confession. (For more information on Catholicism and Catholic concepts which appear in the film, see the section in the chapter on Setting and context, p. 102). He visits Walt several times during the film, making an effort to find him at the bar, visiting him after the first clash with the Hmong gangsters, and trying to keep the police at the Hmong gang house when he is worried that Walt is going to try and take some kind of revenge for the rape of Sue. The young priest is one of the first and last characters to speak in the film at the funerals for Dorothy and Walt respectively.

Father Janovich is persistent. He had promised Dorothy that he would look after Walt when she was gone and that he would take his confession (00:06:50 and 00:07:20, and again at 00:18:15). Despite Walt's constant rudeness and rejection – "I confess that I never cared much for church" (00:07:30) – Father Janovich keeps trying to get through to Walt. He calls him "Walt" in an effort to be friendly and close, but Walt constantly denies him this familiarity, and tells him to call him Mr. Kowalski instead. Walt rejects the priest and the Church and tries to keep a distance between him and them.

The film shows how Father Janovich struggles with his own understanding of his faith and his job (being a priest, the two are very closely connected). The film begins with his rather shallow and, to Walt, annoying comments about "this thing we call life" and the "bittersweet" nature of death for Catholics. As Walt tells him in typically blunt Walt style, the young priest has no understanding of these big issues: "What the hell do you know about life and death?" (00:18:30). He is too young and has too little experience of the world and other people.

By confronting Walt and trying to get him to be a good Catholic and give his confession, Father Janovich finds himself having to dig deeper into his own beliefs. The priest's biggest test comes after the violence (01:27:00). He visits Walt, sees that the old man is plotting some kind of revenge, and has to find a way to stop the violence from continuing. Walt asks him what he thinks he should do, or Thao should do and even what the priest himself would do. He seems to be satisfied with the honesty of the priest's answers and offers him a beer. Father Janovich's persistence with Walt has paid off: the old man respects him now. He asks his advice and listens to what he says. He even tells the priest to call him "Walt" instead of Mr. Kowalski.

Father Kowalksi gets the last word. The film ends with Walt's funeral, and the priest, having become closer to this difficult old man, is able to give a more honest and specific speech than he was for Dorothy. The priest's words definitely show that Walt's tough, rough humor has rubbed off on him: the simple sentimentality of the opening funeral speech is very different from Father Janovich's "and boy, did I learn" here at the end.

Points to remember:

- Janovich is very young and inexperienced, but he is maybe not as naïve and shallow as Walt thinks he is.
- He is loyal (he had promised Dorothy to get Walt's confession) and persistent (he continues to approach Walt despite the latter's rudeness and hostility).

- The priest has a mostly old-aged congregation of white Americans, but he is also involved with social outreach programs which work with the Hmong community.

Key scenes:

- (00:02:25) The first time we see the priest is when he is speaking at Dorothy's funeral. Walt is very unhappy with the shallow and clichéd things the priest says about life and death.
- (00:06:50) At the wake: "How are you holding up, Walt?" "That's Mr. Kowalski." The next time they meet he tries again to call him "Walt" and is again told not to do so.
- (00:07:20) "Dorothy mentioned specifically that it was her desire for you to go to confession."
- (00:11:22) The most quotable and direct scene showing the relationship between Walt and the priest: "Well, I think you're an over-educated, 27-year old virgin who likes to hold the hands of old ladies who are superstitious and promises them eternity." This obviously makes an impression on Father Janovich: he quotes it word for word at Walt's funeral (01:44:38) as he expresses respect for Walt's character and directness.
- (00:17:20) Father Janovich comes to find Walt at the bar and they talk about life and death. Walt shows his contempt for the young priest's lack of experience and understanding. But it is the priest who has the sharpest insight: "It sounds like you know a lot more about death than you do living."
- (00:27:15) After the showdown with the Hmong gangsters, Father Janovich comes to Walt. We learn here that the young priest works with the Hmong gangs as part of the church's social outreach programs. This scene is also the first time that Walt admits to being haunted by things he has done – despite having claimed, in the last conversation with Father Janovich, that he is at peace with what happened during the war.

- (01:27:00) After the shooting and the rape of Sue, Father Janovich comes to see Walt. This very dark (visually and thematically) scene shows us that the priest has grown: he is not trying to "sell" Walt any Catholic rituals or simple solutions. Walt is also not trying to provoke or insult the priest here. The two men treat each other with more honesty. This scene shows us how events have changed both of these characters and their relationship with one another.

Youa

Youa is a Hmong teenage girl. She and Thao obviously like each other: when Walt is at the barbecue in the Lor house, he observes the two of them. Youa makes an effort to talk to Walt, because he is so obviously out of place, and the two have a relaxed and good-humored conversation. She finds him funny and he enjoys talking to her. Walt then harasses Thao for not having the courage to ask her out. Later, Walt learns that Thao did actually ask her out on a date. Youa is at the Lor house, barbecuing with the Lors and Walt (01:22:00). Walt is pleased that the two are going out, and he offers to lend Thao the Gran Torino so he can take her out in style.

Points to remember:

- Youa is a friendly, pretty Hmong girl who becomes Thao's girlfriend.

Key scenes:

- (00:48:00) The first time he visits the Lor house, Walt ends up in a conversation with Youa. They enjoy talking to one another.

Martin

Walt's barber, Martin is an Italian-American with whom Walt trades insults, many of which are racist or homophobic. The two men are friends. When Walt is trying to teach Thao "how guys talk" (01:10:00), he brings him to Martin for instruction and examples.

Martin is presented in the film as a fairly stereotypical "guy": when Walt takes Thao to see him, Martin is sitting around looking at a pornographic magazine. He's set up in the film not as a major, fully rounded character (unlike Sue, for example), but as a representative of a simple idea: this is what a "guy" is. He works. He talks rough. He's not sensitive or politically correct. He doesn't display affection openly. He's an example of the kind of man Walt likes to spend time with.

Martin is one of the places Walt visits on his last afternoon when he is preparing for the end (01:32:00). Walt asks him for a straight shave (something of a luxury) and not only doesn't complain about the price, which is unusual, but gives him twice the price ($20).

Points to remember:

- The barber is Italian-American and he enjoys trading racial insults with Walt.
- Martin is younger than Walt but he shares his rough, offensive humor.
- Walt takes Thao to see Martin for a lesson in "how guys talk".

Key scenes:

- First scene (00:29:00): an introduction to how Walt and Martin talk to one another, showing us the kind of interaction Walt enjoys.
- Second scene (01:10:00): Thao learns "how guys talk" by practicing with Martin and Walt.
- Third scene (01:32:00): Walt visits him to prepare for the end.

Trey

Trey only appears in one scene (00:30:00-00:34:08). He is a white boy who adopts African-American styles of dressing, talking and behavior. He is unable to defend Sue from an aggressive group of young black men and Walt treats him with contempt. (Incidentally, the actor who plays Trey, Scott Eastwood, is Clint Eastwood's youngest son.)

Structure, genre and style

Structure – chronological and symmetrical

The structure of *Gran Torino* is essentially very simple. It follows a chronological narrative: the story it tells is told in the sequence in which it happened, with no flashbacks or experiments. The story has a lot of symmetry, where events and symbols reflect one another.

The chronology of the film covers a period of a few weeks at the end of Walt's life. His wife has just died, and, as he is settling down to life alone as a widower, he becomes involved in the lives of his Hmong neighbors, in particular the two teenagers Sue and Thao. The crisis in the story (Sue being raped after Walt beats up one of the gangsters) is the result of actions Walt has taken – defending the Lor family from the gangsters and beating up one of them – and defines what will happen for the rest of the film.

It begins and ends with events which mirror one another in both very real (Dorothy's funeral, Walt's death) and symbolic forms (one man's life ends and another begins – Walt and Thao, respectively). The tidy symmetry of the film can be found in many elements. For example, the car itself and what it symbolizes are important, especially as the film is given the name of the car. When it belongs to Walt, it is a beloved but immobile object, but at the end of the film, when it has passed on to Thao, we see it moving for the first time and becoming what it is supposed to be. The symmetry includes small details, such as Walt and Grandma Vor mirroring one another as old people sitting on their porches watching the world go by (and spitting) and it also shows the symmetry of the largest things in life (birth and death) with the wake at Walt's house and the Hmong celebration of a new-born baby next door. Some of the symmetries are visual – the horoscope and the shaman, for example, or the funerals – and some are more thematic and symbolic, like the very different father-son relationships between Walt and Mitch and Walt and Thao.

Examples of symmetry	
The films begins with a funeral and Father Janovich speaking about Dorothy	The film ends with a funeral and Father Janovich speaking about Walt
After the funeral there is a wake at Walt's house, a ritual for the dead	At the Hmong house next door the birth of a baby is being celebrated, a ritual for the living
00:11:00 Walt is glaring at Grandma Lor and complaining about his Hmong neighbours in English, a language she doesn't understand. When he has finished, he spits.	Grandma Lor is complaining about Walt in a language he cannot understand. When he spits, she spits.
Walt mimes a gun at the African-Americans as a warning.	Walt mimes a gun at the Hmong as a reminder of how he chased them off.
The Hmong bring Walt flowers and food in gratitude. He rejects them and throws them away. 00:25:10	The Hmong bring flowers and food: Walt is more gracious this time. "Well, OK. Put them over there." 00:51:40
A telephone conversation shows us how bad the relationship is between father and son: Mitch calls Walt 00:21:00	A second telephone conversation shows us again how Walt can't communicate with his son, but the roles are reversed: Walt calls Mitch 00:59:48
Walt's birthday: he is patronized by his son and daughter-in-law and he throws them out of the house.	Walt's birthday: he is welcomed by the Hmong and invited into their house.
Thao asks Walt for help with fixing the kitchen sink.	Walt asks Thao for help carrying the fridge up out of his cellar.

Walt reads his horoscope in the newspaper (00:37:00). This American superstition is mirrored later by the Hmong ritual.	The Hmong shaman (00:44:30) wants to "read" Walt. This ritual is a reflection of the newspaper horoscope: both are examples to foretell the future, more or less seriously.

Steady and careful development

The storytelling in *Gran Torino* is very deliberate: one event or development builds upon what has come before. There are no big jumps or surprises. As an example of how this works in practice, we can look at a series of scenes from the middle of the film, from 00:50:00 to 01:08:00. These scenes cover the growing relationship between Walt and Thao. Walt and Sue have already formed a strong friendship: Thao is a more difficult case.

What we have here is, in order:
- Sue and her mother force Walt to let Thao work for him to make amends for having tried to steal the car.
- Walt is surprised when Thao actually turns up for work.
- Walt watches Thao work: the boy is diligent and works very hard.
- Thao works so well that other neighbours ask Walt if they can have Thao to do things for them.
- Thao is disappointed when the last day of work comes.
- Walt calls his son and fails to connect with him: he is scared about his doctor's results.
- Walt and Thao see the Hmong gangsters driving past in a threatening manner.
- Thao asks Walt for help with their kitchen sink.
- Walt shows Thao how to use tools, and asks about the gangsters.
- Walt asks Thao for help carrying his old freezer. Thao asserts himself against Walt's protests.
- Thao is cleaning the Gran Torino. Sue tells Walt he is like a father to them and says she knows that Walt actually likes Thao.
- Walt talks to Thao about what he wants to do in life.

This is a gradual and efficiently arranged sequence of events, each of them building on what has come before, and this sequence is at the heart of the film. It is these scenes which show us *how* Walt and Thao become close. Through working together, spending time together and earning each other's respect, the two central characters in the film overcome their problems – Walt's contempt for Thao, and Thao's guilt for the attempted theft of the car – and have become, by the time they are talking about Thao's future, something like father and son.

The storytelling in this sequence is methodical. There is no sudden jump from contempt to affection: we see how gradual the process is. By showing us the individual steps the two characters take towards one another, the film makes the overall effect much more convincing. Following a golden rule in storytelling, "show, don't tell", we are not just being *told* that Walt is like a father figure to Thao and Sue: we are being *shown* how this happens. This careful and deliberate style of storytelling is what allows the film to use its story, its narrative, to gradually unfold themes – for example, Walt's racism, masculinity, belonging and community, the meaning of family – which develop and grow with the characters.

The world from Walt's perspective

Walt is the main character. We share his perspective, and we are encouraged to share his personal values, which include impatience with disrespect, laziness, sensitivity and weakness, and respect for the ability of individuals to stand up for themselves and act with strength, confidence and self-sufficiency. To compare and contrast his views, one can point to these relationships in the film:

- Walt respects Sue because she's tough, good-humored and capable of giving as good as she gets in confrontations, but he feels no respect for her white boyfriend because he is weak and helpless.
- He becomes very fond of Thao because he learns that the boy has a good heart and is willing to try as hard as he can, but he dislikes his own grandchildren because they are spoiled and selfish.

- He respects Father Janovich (despite not respecting his beliefs) because of his persistence and loyalty, but he has no respect for his own sons, who he sees as being manipulative and untruthful.

Walt's moral vision becomes ours: the structure of the film and its story shows us the story as Walt sees it, and the redemption he achieves comes in allowing us, the viewers, to see the good in the man beneath his superficially harsh and offensive behavior. The structure of the film is methodical, patient and systematic. Bit by bit we learn more about how Walt reacts to other people, and how much of his rough personality is a bit of a show, theatrical in away, as opposed to being deeply felt. Walt's racism is a complex topic, and the structure of the film and the way the story is told allows us to get beneath the surface of his offensive attitudes to see something larger and stronger beneath (see the chapter on Themes in this study guide for more on Walt's moral code, p. 87).

Genre and sub-genre

Gran Torino is a drama. While it does include gangsters, attempted grand theft auto and shootings, it could not be classified as a crime movie, gangster film or thriller – none of the elements of these genres are dominant enough to define the film. It's about an old man and his friendship with a young boy, not about gangs and crime. It does, however, belong to a specific sub-genre: it is a vigilante film, even if it happens to be an unusual example of the type.

The vigilante film

A vigilante is someone who takes the law into their own hands. The police cannot or will not deal with an injustice, for whatever reason, so the vigilante must. The comic book character Batman is the perfect example of a vigilante.

This is a classic Clint Eastwood topic. Many of his films have been about vigilantes and vigilante justice (see Chapter 1.2: The Filmmakers in this study guide for more on Eastwood's career, p. 7). A vigilante is almost always presented as a positive figure, however controversial his or her methods may be, and however much the vigilante's behavior, motivations and acts may contradict the laws and expectations of society. A vigilante story is a way to release pressure: the pressure of feeling frustrated by the slow, incompetent or inadequate efforts of the legal system to handle a society which is seen as being dangerous and chaotic, and which is threatened by forces of violence and evil.

Politically, vigilante stories are extremely popular with conservative and right-wing thinkers. Vigilantes in Western societies are by their very nature anti-liberal: a vigilante is often motivated by impatience and frustration with liberal laws which protect criminals or suspects. A vigilante will take on the role of judge, jury and executioner. The simple black-and-white moral definitions of one individual (the vigilante) can mean life or death for his or her targets. One useful way to think about classic vigilantes is that they see themselves as cleaning up society's rubbish – getting their hands dirty and taking care of things that mainstream society is too scared or squeamish to deal with.

But despite this simple appeal to a brutal, simplistic idea of "justice", vigilantes are always outsiders. They are always individuals who are unable to return to normal society. Their actions are illegal, possibly immoral, and always controversial. The pleasure a vigilante film provides for its audience is vicarious (something which is felt or experienced by watching or reading about it, not by experiencing it oneself). We watch a vigilante dealing with bad guys and while we may enjoy the satisfaction of seeing swift, uncomplicated justice being done, we also know that what we are watching is incompatible with the laws and values of a modern society based on the rule of law and the rights of the individual.

Why *Gran Torino* is such an unusual vigilante film

The vigilantism of Walt in *Gran Torino* is a little different, however. Walt does not storm into the gang's house and begin shooting the bad guys, like the vigilante antiheroes do in the most famous examples of the sub-genre: for example in Eastwood's own *Dirty Harry* (1971), *Taxi*

Driver (starring Robert de Niro, 1976) and *Death Wish* (1974, starring Charles Bronson). Walt is looking to end the cycle of violence in a more complete and final way, which has unmistakable and unavoidable echoes of Christianity and Jesus dying on the Cross. Walt literally offers himself up as a sacrifice so that Thao and Sue can be free.

By sacrificing himself by forcing the gangbangers to kill him in front of witnesses, he is removing the threat they represent by letting them incriminate themselves, and at the same time making it impossible for them to continue to respond with violence in the future by being dead himself. Additionally, his act of vigilantism is unique in that it provides salvation for him, and not just the satisfaction of revenge. The spiritual aspect to Walt's vigilantism is very unusual. While he is not religiously motivated – he is not a soldier of God bringing divine vengeance to those who do evil – the fact that his vigilante act involves him sacrificing himself raises issues of a moral and spiritual nature which the viewer cannot ignore.

Style – broad humor and tough-guy sentimentality

For a film with such a grim and sad story, *Gran Torino* has unexpected flashes of humor, and it also displays a lot of what we can call "tough guy sentimentality". Walt's sentimentality is not expressed in a love of cute things and emotional expressions. It is instead characterized by its silence and lack of expression. He never tells Thao that he likes him, or even that he respects him. The boy comes to feel this, however, through Walt's actions. Once again, we see the principle of "show, don't tell" in action. When Walt does express approval or affection, the gesture actually means something.

Humor

From the spitting contest between Walt and the grandmother to Walt's half-drunken and completely unprovoked harassment of Thao for not having seized his opportunity with Youa (00:45:00), the film has comical moments. This humor is usually broad (unsubtle), which makes it earthy and appropriate for Walt's unpretentious, working-class nature.

When Walt and Thao have established their father-son relationship (following the scenes in which Thao is working for Walt), Walt tells Thao it's time "to man you up". This process is not entirely serious. What we first see is Walt and Martin the barber trying to teach Thao how to be rude and insensitive: this scene (01:10:00) is intended as comedy and played as comedy. For example, Martin and Walt tell Thao that talking like a man means complaining about and insulting people who aren't there: your boss, your car, your wife:

Thao: "But I don't have a job, a car or a girlfriend."

Martin: "Jesus Christ. I should have blown his head off when I had the chance."

There is a lot of teasing in the film, mostly between Walt and Sue and Walt and Martin, but also, as their relationship grows, between Walt and Thao. Note how names are used – Walt constantly calls Thao "Toad" and Sue calls Walt "Wally". This teasing is another example of a humorous touch in the film.

However serious and emotionally deep the film may get, there is always space for moments of humor. When Walt suddenly appears in the church and tells Father Janovich he is there to make his confession (01:32:00), the priest's first reaction is a very un-priestly "Oh Jesus, what have you done?" It may be dark humor, but it is humor, and a very human moment.

Camera work, editing and soundtrack

A common piece of advice for writers is that good style is like good breeding; it never calls attention to itself. This is very much true of Clint Eastwood's approach to directing.

Like the structure of the story and the film, which is clear and unpretentious, the camera work in the film is done without tricks or special effects.

The editing is unhurried: many scenes are left to linger for a second or so to allow us to read more of a character's expression, or for a particular atmosphere to leave an impression on us as viewers. There is no hectic cutting to provide an artificial or exaggerated sense of drama or danger or chaos.

The soundtrack is not intrusive: most of the film has no soundtrack music at all. The few moments which do have a musical soundtrack use a minimal selection of music to emphasise an impression or atmosphere.

Generally speaking, the methods the film uses to tell its story are like the storytelling itself – tidy and efficient, unhurried and unpretentious.

Camera work and editing

The camera work and editing in *Gran Torino* can be characterized by one word: patience. The camera never runs. When it moves, it moves at an unhurried speed. The editing is never hectic or chaotic. This a story about an old man gradually coming to terms with new things in his life (being alone after his wife's death, feeling alienated from his family, making new friends with his Hmong neighbors), and the overall impression of calm and mature observation in the camera work supports the story by reflecting Walt's pace of life.

Here are a couple of examples of how to interpret the use of the camera in specific scenes.

One notable exception to the "no tricks" camera work in the film comes at 01:26:30. After seeing that Sue has been beaten and raped by the gangsters, Walt goes back to his house. In the kitchen he starts punching the cabinets: one of his punches, the third one, suddenly flies directly into the camera. We then see him punching through glass on a kitchen cupboard. This simple trick uses perspective to give the viewer a shock, as we see Walt's fist flying towards us. The effect is to make us more nervous and convinced of the anger and pain in this scene.

Following the rule "less is more", this trick shot is all the more effective because it is the only time in the film the camera takes such an aggressive attitude towards us, the viewers.

At 01:27:00 we have an example of how camera work and lighting can be used to emphasize the meaning and atmosphere of a scene. Father Janovich has come to see Walt after the shooting and the rape. Walt has been sitting alone in the dark. When the two men talk, their faces are half-lit by light coming in from the night-time street and half sunk in shadows. The effect is to make the characters seem more stripped down, which perfectly underlines this conversation, in which they talk to each other more honestly than ever before. There is no posturing or provocation here, and the priest does not try to convince Walt with Christian clichés. There is a sense of extremity – they are talking about life and death and revenge and the possibility of killing people – and emotional nakedness, as they are finally honest with one another.

Soundtrack

We can look at the soundtrack to *Gran Torino* in two separate categories – diegetic and non-diegetic.

Diegetic music and sound is what characters within the film can (or could) hear – the music we hear when we see the organist in the church (00:02:20) is an example of diegetic music, because it is what the characters in the film are also hearing.

Non-diegetic music and sound is music the characters can't hear: it is only for us, the audience. This includes all the rest of the music in the film: the military drumming and the song "Gran Torino", for example.

Diegetic soundtrack

This mostly consists of the music in the church and the rap music the Hmong gangsters listen to.

The organ being played in the church does not tell us anything we did not know already: this is a religious ceremony, a funeral. It provides a little extra color to the scene to establish the seriousness of the ceremony – this helps to highlight how inappropriate and disrespectful the behavior of Walt's grandchildren is.

The gangsters – Chicano as well as Hmong – listen to rap music when they are driving around. This music is ethnically-specific: the Latino gangsters are listening to Spanish-language rap ("Esta es guerra" by Neiver Alvarez), and the Hmong listen to "Hmoob Tuag Nthi" by Elvis Thao, and "All My Hmong Muthafuckaz" by Buddah, for example. This use of diegetic music reinforces the ethnic divisions in the film and the ethnic nature of the gangs. It also provides a more modern, aggressive, threatening and urban sound to balance the films non-diegetic soundtrack and to illustrate the strange modern world around Walt, a character who is very much lost in the past.

Non-diegetic soundtrack

This is the music which is only for us, the audience. This music is used to enhance or emphasize atmospheres and feelings in particular scenes. It is another technical and artistic tool for the filmmaker, like the use of the camera, how the lighting is arranged, or the way the scenes are cut together (editing).

The film's soundtrack was written by Kyle Eastwood (Clint Eastwood's son) and Michael Stevens (who has worked on many of Eastwood's films), and British jazz singer Jamie Cullum, who also wrote the lyrics to the title song.

The soundtrack is very minimal. Instead of a typical Hollywood orchestral soundtrack, which often includes a near-constant carpet of music which swells and accelerates according to the action on the screen, and which also often includes musical themes to identify and announce specific major characters, *Gran Torino* uses only three musical "colors":

- the piano jazz of the title song,
- a military drumbeat,

- and the tense sound of stringed instruments maintaining a constant, high note.

These elements are used very subtly in the film to emphasize the action or atmosphere on screen. The music only takes precedence over what is on screen – that is, we do not hear the actual thing we are watching, only the music – on two occasions. The first is the scene in which Walt watches Thao work (from 00:56:30) and the other is at the end of the film, when we watch Thao and Daisy driving along the lake in the Gran Torino. On both occasions we hear versions of the title song.

The film opens with the softly played piano chords of the song *Gran Torino*. The film uses a lot of tidy symmetry, and this song both opens and closes the film. It creates an atmosphere of melancholy and nostalgia.

Military drumming, enhancing tension, is used when Walt is woken by Thao's fumbled burglary at 00:20:00. The sound itself immediately suggests the military, implying guns, violence, and killing. When we see Walt grab his rifle the sense of tension increases.

"Ain't she sweet," Walt says to Daisy as he admires his Gran Torino (00:22:30), and the title song is playing softly over this scene.

00:55:00 – There is a different tone in the music while Thao is working for Walt: an improvised version of the basic musical elements of the title song creates an emotional, aspirational mood. It suggests the emotional warmth which is growing between Walt and Thao.

01:20:20 – The military drumming comes back as Walt is observing the Hmong gangsters. We by now clearly associate this music with the idea of Walt as a soldier, as a trained killer. The music creates tension and a sense of expectation. We are watching a trained military man as he observes his enemies and plans how to proceed.

01:23:00 – After the drive-by shooting the music is used to create a different kind of tension. Walt doesn't know whether someone in the Lor house has been hurt by the gunfire. The music consists of strings, relatively high-pitched, and the impression it gives is that something bad is about to happen: the tone of the music makes the viewer feel expectant. It comes and goes through the scene, reinforcing this idea that something is about to happen, even as we (and the characters) learn more about what has actually happened, and that Sue is missing.

The high notes are held by the instruments, not providing any sense of release in a melody or a musical climax of any kind. This is a different kind of tension from the atmosphere created by the military drumbeat. It is an uncomfortable and menacing atmosphere.

01:40:00 – Walt's sacrificial death is accompanied, after the shooting, by the soft piano and voice of the song *Gran Torino*, which also opened the film.

The title song was nominated for a Golden Globe Award. It was written and performed by Clint Eastwood, who is famous for his love of jazz and is also an accomplished piano player.

Themes, imagery and symbolism

In this section the themes, imagery and symbolism used in the film are identified and interpreted, with examples to show how these techniques are used to tell the story, and how the characters affect and are affected by the development of these larger ideas about people, life, community and behavior.

Many of these themes are closely connected to one another: for example, it is important to pay attention to how Walt's increased sense of **belonging** to his new "family" of Thao and Sue affects his **racism**, and how Walt's ideas about **masculinity** help Thao become less of an **outsider**. The theme of **violence** is also deeply connected to the theme of **masculinity**, for example, and is central to the theme of **sacrifice** because of how Walt chooses to break the cycle.

Race, racism and immigration

- Racial hierarchies in American society
- Racism and sexuality
- How a theme can develop: Walt's racism

Religious themes

- Confession: guilt and forgiveness
- Sacrifice and redemption

Belonging

- Forms of belonging
  - family
  - community
  - gangs
- Things which help us belong
  - community rituals
  - rites of passage
  - food
  - status symbols
- The people who don't belong
  - outsiders

Walt's moral code

Masculinity

- Patriarchal Hmong culture

- Walt's example
- The gang: predators
- Emasculation
- A man and his tools
- Homophobia

The cycle of violence

- Guns, and the threat of guns
- The rape

The Gran Torino

- As an object of desire
- The past and the future
- The DVD special feature documentaries

Changes

- Urban demographics
- Second chances

Omens

Race, racism and immigration

The issue of race and racism is a dominant theme in the film. Walt's racism is one of his most striking features. The various characters in the film are all defined by their race or ethnicity – the Polish-Americans, Martin the Italian-American barber, the Hmong, the Chicano gangbangers, the African-American youth. Walt's language is filled with racially-charged words and phrases, most of them abusive, and he loves telling racist jokes (00:17:20). He is obviously uncomfortable in the doctor's office (00:59:00) where he is surrounded by non-white Americans. His own son is embarrassed by his racism (00:08:00): Mitch drives a Hyundai – Walt says: "Would it have killed you to buy American?" Mitch complains afterwards to his wife: "Did you see the way he looked at the truck? It's always rice burner this, Jap burner that."

Race is a great dividing issue in the film. Walt is a white racist, and he talks and behaves as if white Americans of European descent are better than non-white people. Part of it stems from fear (fighting an Asian enemy in Korea, losing his community to outsiders) and part of it comes from a need to demarcate the world or community he belongs to (his white world) from the unknown world (black, Asian, Hispanic communities). The need to have a sense of belonging often leads to racism, as people develop a feeling of "us and them".

There is a hierarchy of racism in American society which the film touches on, and an uncomfortable sexual element to racial stereotypes which *Gran Torino* also points out. But most relevantly when interpreting the film, *Gran Torino* shows the development of this theme in the character of Walt, as he gets to know the Lor family better, becoming more involved in their lives, and his racist and offensive attitudes begin to change. Becoming familiar with the unfamiliar allows him to have a more ambiguous attitude to the changes taking place in his neighborhood.

The characters of various ethnic background in the film are:

Walt and his family – Polish-American
Father Janovich – Polish-American
Martin the barber – Italian-American
Tim Kennedy – the Irish-American supervisor at the construction site
The various Hmong characters, from first generation immigrants with no English (the grandmother) to the integrated third generation characters (Sue and Thao, who are Hmong-Americans)
The Chicano (Mexican-American) gangsters
The African-Americans who harass Sue and her boyfriend
The multi-racial group of people in the waiting room at the doctor's office, the black Muslim nurse and Asian-American doctor

Racial hierarchies in American society

Walt talks about being "American" in a way that ignores the essential fact of the USA, which is that it is a nation built by immigrants. As an elderly Polish-American, he looks down on the Asian-Americans and African-Americans around him, but forgets (or ignores) that his grandfather's and father's generation would have been treated equally badly by the European Protestant Americans who thought that the Catholic immigrants – the Irish, Italians and Poles – were a plague of uncivilized, filthy, superstitious barbarians.

- To use examples from cinema, both Francis Ford Coppola's *Godfather* films (especially *The Godfather II*, 1974) and Martin Scorsese's *Gangs of New York* (2002) show how Catholic immigrants were discriminated against by all other white demographic groups in the USA during the 19th and early 20th centuries.
- The history of the Mafia in American is rooted in the discrimination against Catholic Italian immigrants, which led to them living in poverty in ghettoes and having to rely on almost tribal gang structures from the old world (Sicily) to defend their families and businesses. When the Mafia became more predatory and criminally-inclined, it continued to be most active within the Catholic Italian immigrant community, because this community was so discriminated against and isolated in ghettoes and was unwilling or unable to look to the police for help.
- The social discrimination of Catholic Polish immigrants is also covered in books like Upton Sinclair's *The Jungle* (1906), which sensationally exposed the appalling living and working conditions of the Poles in Chicago's meat industry in the early 20th century.
- A famous example of a Polish character in American literature is the working-class Stanley Kowalski in Tennessee Williams' play *A Streetcar Named Desire*. This character is more complex than Walt, but shares with him a working-class, macho attitude. The play is set in New Orleans, right across the country from Detroit, but both Walt and Stanley illustrate the typical working-class existence of Polish immigrants, even in later generations.
- Closer to the reality of Detroit, the first generation of workers in the new car factories in the early 20th century were poor immigrants from South and East European Catholic countries. These immigrants were only wanted for their cheap labor, and because it was easy for powerful companies like the Ford Motor Company to exploit them. When strict immigration laws were enforced and American society turned against poor, unskilled immigrants from Europe and Asia, these workers were pushed out in favor of African-Americans from the South of the USA – another socially unwanted, but economically convenient source of labor.

The dominant demographic in the USA when it comes to power, money, influence and social status has always been, and mostly remains, what are called WASPs – White Anglo-Saxon Protestants. For them, Catholics were lower-class citizens from poor countries and were not treated as equals. The same pattern of behavior repeats itself throughout society: groups defined by ethnic or religious belonging will typically find a way to look down on another group. In current American society, for example, Muslims and ethnic groups from the Middle East are the groups most others look at with suspicion or dislike, and immigrants and refugees from South and Central American countries are subject to consistently high levels of prejudice and discrimination.

These prejudices are likely to remain, because they are not limited exclusively to race (ethnicity or skin color) or religion. They have a lot to do with social status – rich or successful people will often be forgiven for the things which will land poor people in trouble. When Sue tells Walt that Hmong girls tend to go to college while the boys go to jail, she is talking about a social problem that makes the racial problem worse. In a vicious cycle of poverty and social discrimination, the expectation of hopelessness is reinforced by experience for young Hmong boys like Thao whose only visible male role models are gangsters or elderly relatives who cannot speak English and seem to live in the past.

Racism and sexuality

In addition to the complicating influences of social status and acceptance on the issue of racism, there is also often a disturbing sexual element to racial prejudice and abuse. This is relevant to *Gran Torino*. The Chicano gangsters taunt Thao by saying they do not know whether he is a boy or a girl, repeating a widespread racist stereotype that Asian men are effeminate – Walt also refers to Thao's "little girl hands" (01:05:44). The black youths who harass Sue are, as she loudly points out, almost comically conforming to racial and sexual stereotypes of African-American men fetishizing Asian girls. The three young men emasculate her boyfriend (deny him any masculinity) by pushing him out of the way when they begin to harass Sue. The filmmakers here exploit an ancient white racist fear of the sexual potency of black men.

These examples are preparing us for what will be the real crisis of the film, the moment which proves to be a turning point in the lives of all the characters: the rape of Sue by the members of the Hmong gang, which is the use of sexuality as a weapon to hurt, humiliate and provoke.

How a theme can develop: Walt and his racism

The theme of racism is not static in *Gran Torino*. It changes, just as Walt himself changes. Providing more evidence for the theory that one of the most important sources of racism is ignorance, we see that the more Walt gets to know Sue and Thao and the Hmong culture, the less antagonistic and abusive he is. But even here Walt is an interesting and complex example: Walt's racism is not only about hatred. As his relationship with Martin the barber shows, Walt enjoys the provocation of offensive and insensitive language, which today is usually called non-politically correct (non-PC). His racism is active on different levels: there appears to be a genuine, and genuinely unpleasant, level of racial hatred. But layered on top of that is what we can call Walt's "theatrical racism".

Banter: This is a very good word to use when describing the kind of conversation Walt Kowalski obviously enjoys. Banter is friendly remarks and jokes. It can be used as both a noun ("He enjoyed the banter") and a verb ("She was bantering with her aunt"). A bantering conversation is one which goes back and forth. Walt and Martin throw things at one another, and Sue responds to Walt without getting offended: Walt has bantering conversations with both of them.

When Walt tells racist jokes with his cronies at the bar, or trades racist insults with his barber, or teases Sue about Hmong culture and history, he is still being racist – implying that people of some races are better, more important or more valuable than people of other races. But there is an undeniable element of self-awareness: there is a line, however thin and however blurred, between outright racist abuse and teasing. There is an element of theatricality to a lot of Walt's racist statements. He knows that what he is saying is not politically correct, and *he likes it that way*. He enjoys provoking reactions: either the tit-for-tat banter he gets from Martin and Sue, or the shocked indignation of his family members. He's not saying silly racist things for any other reason than to provoke.

We can see in his interactions with Sue that he's also more than happy to take it in return: "I am. I'm the white devil," he says (01:22:30) when Sue warns Youa to stay away from him. This is a more significant example of the kind of racist banter between Walt and Martin, both of whom are white and of European ethnicities. He feels comfortable enough among the Hmong by this point to laugh at himself and his own theatrical racist nonsense.

Racial slurs used in the film

All of the words listed below are, of course, words that should never be used to describe people of other races – they are offensive and insulting.

Some of them are crude and brutally basic descriptors:

- *slope*, for example, refers to the slanted eyes many Asian people have.
- *chink* and *nip* refer to Chinese and Japanese people (*Nippon* is the Japanese word for Japan).
- *beaner* became a term of abuse for Mexicans due to the widespread use of beans in Mexican cooking
- Walt also calls Thao egg roll (*Art Frühlingsrolle*), another food reference used as a lazy and pointless racial slur, but here it seems to be Walt's invention.

Others refer to deeper and older racist stereotypes which assume that all people of a particular ethnicity share certain (usually negative) characteristics.

- *dragon lady* is a persistent racist stereotype of Asian women as being dangerous and mysterious.
- *jew* as a verb means "to steal" and is particularly offensive. It draws on centuries of anti-Semitic stereotypes and myths about Jews and their relationship to money.

- *honky* and *spook* are specifically American. *Honky* was first adopted as a term of abuse for white people by the Black Power civil rights movement in the 1960s: its origins are unknown. *Spook* has been used as a white racist insult for African-Americans since at least the 1940s.

The following are used by Walt: (for Asians) *gook, swamp rats, fish heads, zipperhead, egg roll, slopes*; (for Asian women) *dragon lady*; (for African-Americans) *spooks*; *jew* (meaning to steal), (for Martin, an Italian-American) *doo-wop dago*; (for Irish) *Mick*; (for Mexicans) *beaners*; (for poor whites) *white trash hillbilly*; (for himself) *white devil.*

The following are used by Martin: (for Polish) *Polack*; (for Asians) *chink, nip, gook.*

The following is used by young African-American man to Walt: *honky*

Religious themes

The film begins and ends with scenes in the church and with the priest speaking. Religious themes of confession and sacrifice are strong in the story. One of the main relationships which evolves through the film is that between Walt and Father Janovich, and we see several scenes where the two men talk about religious issues.

Walt is a test of faith for Father Janovich. The old man is rude to him personally, and also rejects his authority and role as a priest (00:18:00: the scene in the bar for a good example of how Walt criticizes the priest's ideas). The young priest has made a promise, though, and he continues to make an effort to do his duty as a Catholic priest and look out for one of his congregation, even if this particular member is Walt Kowalski.

Religion is a strong presence in the film for two main reason: firstly, the promise Father Janovich made to Dorothy to get Walt to go to confession, and the young priest's determination to keep that promise; and secondly, the way in which Walt breaks the cycle of violence, which is unmistakably Christ-like in its combination of non-violence, sacrifice and love enabling others to be free.

Confession: guilt and forgiveness

We only learn towards the end of the film the nature of the guilt Walt carries around with him, and why it is has poisoned him and made him so dark, angry and cold (01:36:00). But we can see that Dorothy knew it was there, the priest sees that there is something there, and the Hmong shaman sees it in him, too. Walt has to confess this guilt, to get it out from inside himself, in order to be free: but he does not choose the Catholic structure to do this. His confession to Father Janovich (01:33:00) is genuine in a way, but he is also mocking the priest. The sins he confesses to Father Janovich are not lies, but they are also not relevant to the real issues. The real confession he makes is to Thao (01:36:00).

The Catholic Church and Father Janovich's status and authority as a priest mean nothing to Walt. He makes this very clear. He does not care about the confession apart from wanting to make sure that the priest gets to keep his promise and making his dead wife's wish come true. His relationship with Thao is more real to him, more valuable, and more important. His confession to Thao about the guilt he feels allows him to explain to the boy, even if he does not immediately understand it, why he has to stop the violence. It does not seem that Walt is particularly interested in forgiveness – he does not want a higher authority to tell him that everything is OK. What he does do, though, is to make sure that his guilt, the burden he has carried, is used for something good and useful – specifically keeping Thao from making a stupid mistake and either getting killed or killing someone else.

Staying true to his character as a man of few words, Walt would rather let his actions speak for him than just have a conversation with a priest. Walt is not looking for forgiveness: he is looking for redemption.

Sacrifice and redemption

Despite openly and rudely rejecting the priest, the Church and religion in general, Walt's actions at the end of the film unmistakably imitate the example of Jesus Christ – the sacrifice of self for the good of others.

One of the major changes in the message of the Bible between the Old Testament (before Jesus) and the New Testament (which covers the life of Jesus) concerns how to deal with violence. The two relevant quotations are very famous:

And thine eye shalt not pity: life for life, eye for eye, tooth for tooth, hand for hand, foot for foot. (Deuteronomy 19:21)

You have heard that it was said, "An eye for an eye and a tooth for a tooth." But I say to you, Do not resist the one who is evil. But if anyone slaps you on the right cheek, turn to him the other also. (Matthew 5:38–39)

The first idea is also called *lex talionis* (Latin for "the law of talion") and it encourages revenge under the law. It demands that anyone who commits a crime of offence against another person should have the same thing done to them in revenge.

The second example is a message of non-violence. It comes from the Sermon on the Mount, the most important collection of the moral teachings of Jesus in the New Testament. It is most often referred to in everyday conversation as "turning the other cheek", which means *not* retaliating, and *not* taking revenge.

One reason why the example of Jesus' death on the Cross is so important is that it is a symbolic act of non-violence which breaks the cycle of violence. A famous saying goes, "Violence is always a question and never an answer", which means that reacting to violence with more violence will always in turn demand more violence: a vicious circle. Walt learns this in *Gran Torino* when he sees what happens after he beats up Smokie in revenge for the gang having beaten up Thao: the gang does a drive-by shooting and kidnaps and rapes Sue. The "eye for an eye" approach to the conflict is not working. It is very obviously only making everything worse.

Walt thinks long and hard about what he should do. He feels responsible, and he wants to save Sue and Thao from any more danger from the Hmong gang. He has learned that violence will not help.

Combine this with two other important factors: his sense of guilt, both for his past and for what has happened to Sue; and the fact that he is alone, old, near the end of his life, and dying anyway. Walt makes the decision to sacrifice himself in a way which will force the gang to kill him: his death will be the mechanism which allows the gang to be destroyed, not by killing them, but by having them commit murder in front of witnesses. He can redeem himself by performing an act of sacrifice and goodness which will help others (Thao and Sue) live in peace and freedom.

Many ideas in the film come together at the end, including even Walt's ability to provoke other people with his offensive racism: he provokes the gang members into being angry, and he keeps provoking them and challenging them until they shoot him when he tries to put his hand in his pocket.

He has kept all his promises and tidied up everything that is left in his life, including making sure that his dog Daisy has a new home, and he intentionally lets himself be killed. Despite Walt not being religious, this is a religious act of sacrifice. He saves Thao and Sue, and he redeems himself.

Key scenes:

- (00:07:30) "I confess that I never really cared for church very much. The only reason I went was because of [Dorothy]. And I confess that I have no desire to confess to a boy that's just out of the seminary." This is one of several useful quotations from early in the film to show how much contempt Walt has for religion, the Church and the young priest.
- (00:28:15) "It seems it would do you good to unload some of that burden." Father Janovich makes another attempt to get Walt to come to confession. Walt dismisses and mocks the idea of salvation here.
- (01:30:00) Walt goes to see Father Janovich to give his confession. Walt keeps his promise, and makes sure the priest keeps his, too. This is part of him tying up loose ends before he dies. He doesn't want to leave a mess when he dies.
- (01.37:00) Walt tells Thao the truth about what haunts him, getting a medal of valour for killing a Korean kid who wanted to surrender – this is a key moment for Walt, and this scene is his real, honest act of confession.

- (01:41:00) The image of Walt lying dead with arms outstretched is a reference to Jesus on the Cross. This Christ symbolism effectively shows that despite being anti-religious, Walt has learned the lessons of Jesus' message of love and non-violence and used them to save his friends Sue and Thao.

Belonging

The theme of belonging is large and complex. Characters belong (or do not belong) to ethnic groups, social classes, families, religious congregations, and other groups. This belonging is not always voluntary. Walt, for example, evidently does not enjoy belonging to his family. Forms of belonging which are enforced by tradition or blood can be given up in favor of a more emotional and in a sense "real" belonging. Walt gives up on his family to become a part of the lives of his Hmong neighbors, in particular Thao. At the end, it is the Hmong who inherit from him, and not his white family. And because the concept of belonging by definition will always mean that there are others who do not belong, the film includes outsiders, those who for whatever reason cannot or will not belong to particular groups.

The idea of belonging is not simple. It changes constantly as surroundings and situations change, and this idea of change, central to the story of *Gran Torino*, is important to the theme of belonging.

Forms of belonging:
Family: the families we are born into and the families we choose
Community: ethnicity and neighborhood; religion and tradition
Gangs: masculinity, social outsiders, peer pressure, ethnicity

Things which help us belong:
Community rituals: funerals, births, birthdays, family gatherings, customs, the rituals of politeness, rites of passage
Food
Status symbols

The people who do not belong:
Outsiders who are not part of your community, culture, etc.

Forms of belonging

Family

The theme of family is very ambiguous in *Gran Torino*. We can find very positive and very negative opinions and ideas but no simple black-and-white expression of what the film thinks family is, or what family is good for.

On the negative side, we have Walt's own family and Thao's cousin Fong. You cannot help who you are related to: Walt very clearly does not like or respect his own sons and their families. Sue Lor makes it equally plain that she doesn't like or respect or trust her gangster cousin Fong ("Spider").

Walt's dislike of his own sons is mirrored by their impatience with him and their inability to understand him. It becomes obvious during the film that they see Walt as a problem that has to be solved, and the best solution they have for him is to try to put him in an assisted living facility (Mitch: "It's like staying in a hotel, practically! […] They take care of everything, they clean up", 00:39:55). On the surface they appear to have good intentions: he is old, and they worry that he will have a hard time living alone in a neighborhood which has changed a lot in recent years. But as Walt understands it – and we as viewers can share his interpretation – they simply want to put him away somewhere where he cannot cause trouble and he can be someone else's problem.

The theme of family is not easy for Thao, either. He is a gentle and introspective boy. He does not have the aggression and dominant personality expected of a man, and the women in his family, as well as the Hmong gangsters, are disappointed that he obeys his sister so much and does not behave in a more traditionally "manly" fashion.

On the negative side of things, we also have the pressure Fong puts on Thao, as his cousin, to join their gang.

The positive side is seen in how Sue and Thao stick together, and how the Hmong family, while being frustrating for someone like Thao who is struggling to find his identity and his place in the world, does provide reliable and comforting structures and customs.

But family is not defined just by blood relations. Late in his life Walt finds a new family in the Lors. A very strong symbolic bond in the film is the role Walt and Thao play for each other as surrogate father and son, and he very clearly has an equally strong paternal relationship, combined with a very strong sense of respect, with Sue Lor. Sue says this very clearly (01:04:00), telling Walt he is like a father for Thao (and her).

There is no man in the Lor family, we learn at the beginning. Thao is expected to fill the role of man in the house, but his personality does not fit in well with the Hmong's patriarchal traditions. His sister Sue is much more forceful and tough, and acts, as we see in the film, as the family's spokesperson: she is more fluent in English than her mother and grandmother, and more able to stand up to and confront outsiders and challenges than her brother. Walt's role as father figure to the Lor children is one of the most important devices in the film, providing an emotional context as well as a motivation for the narrative.

To support this theme of belonging to a family and specifically finding a family, one small scene is particularly significant. Walt has a moment of clarity when he is at the Lor house. After the encounter with the Lor shaman he speaks to his own reflection in the bathroom mirror, saying "I have more in common with these gooks than I do with my own spoilt rotten family" (00:46:00).

This moment of self-awareness, together with his already-established relationship with Sue and the more complex relationship he will build with Thao, is the key to Walt's second chance in life. He faces up to who he truly is as he approaches death, and this second family, a more true family in a way, based as it is on love and respect rather than the coincidence of birth, is what is most important to him.

Key scenes:

- The problems between Walt and his sons are covered in several scenes throughout the film, most importantly the two telephone calls (Mitch calls Walt (00:21:00) and Walt calls Mitch (00:59:48)), the birthday visit with brochures for the old people's home (00:38:36), and Walt's confession to Father Janovich that "I was never very close with my two sons" (01:33:45).
- (00:09:15) Thao listens while his grandmother and a male relative talk about whether or not he is enough of a man.

- (00:15:30) Sue's reactions to her cousin: "Spider? Is that what he just called you – *Fong*?" She doesn't like Fong and doesn't want him to have anything to do with Thao. They are cousins, family – she knows who he really is and finds his tough-guy gangster act ridiculous.
- (01:07:00) In this very important scene Sue tells Walt how important he has become for her and for Thao – as a role model, and as a father figure. She says that she wishes their own father had been more like Walt.

Community

When Walt defends the Lor family from the gangsters (00:22:55) he is acting as a member of a community – this time it is a community of neighbors. At the beginning communities were organized along ethnic lines, but Walt takes action here to defend his neighbors and his own property. After this night he is overwhelmed by gratitude and attention from the Hmong people and is increasingly drawn into the lives of the Lor family.

The neighborhood community theme is evident in how Thao and Walt help each other (from 01:01:00). Thao needs Walt's help fixing the tap in the kitchen, and Walt needs Thao's help getting rid of his fridge. They help each other because they are neighbors. By this point, the racial problems (for Walt) and fear and shyness (for Thao) have almost completely gone. By living next to each other, working together and learning to respect one another, Walt and Thao are displaying how neighborhood communities function. They have also become almost famous in the neighborhood as a team who can get things fixed: other neighbors come to ask Walt if he can have Thao fix stuff for them (00:57:30).

The reflections of communities based around ritual are found throughout the film – the Catholics and the Hmong are the most obvious examples of this, with the juxtaposition at the film's beginning of the funeral and the celebrations of a birth. There is a gathering at the beginning for the funeral and wake, and there is another kind of congregation at the end of the film, with the gangsters, the Lor family, the neighbors and the police, gathered to witness the death of Walt Kowalski. Both congregations witness death. The first, more formal congregation is witnessing Dorothy Kowalski's passing, and the final congregation witnesses Walt's sacrifice and death. A final congregation is for Walt's funeral.

Gangs

A negative aspect of the theme of belonging involves the ethnic gangs in the film. Thao is under enormous pressure from his cousin and the other Hmong gangsters to "belong". They cannot understand why he prefers being alone and why he does what his sister tells him. The gang represents a peculiarly twisted image of community, and also of masculinity: this is a world of crime and violence, where all that matters is fighting with people who look different – blacks, whites, Latinos – and conforming to a very specific and brutal idea of what it means to be a man. Thao's gentle, cautious and introverted nature makes him very unsuited for this world.

The other thing we see in the film is that the gangs are clearly organized around ethnicity. The soundtrack to the film includes gangsta rap songs by Hmong-ethnic artists which are very specifically aimed at an exclusively Hmong-American audience (see the chapter in this study guide on Camera work, editing and soundtrack for more on the songs used, p. 63).

Things which help us belong

Community rituals

Community rituals are about finding meaning in the events of life which unite all people: birth, passing into adulthood, marriage and death. *Gran Torino* is very interested in these events, in particular what death can mean and what it means to be a man (an adult).

The beginning of the film offers a comparison between two communities involved in traditional rituals: the Polish-American Catholics attend a funeral and then a wake, and the Hmong next door to Walt have a large family gathering to celebrate the birth of a child. Both rituals – the wake and the blessing – involve family gatherings and lots of food.

These opening scenes in the film are significant for the themes of *Gran Torino*.

- We can see here that, despite all the superficial differences, families and tribes and people of different cultures tend to celebrate in the same way: by gathering with those close to them, sharing comfort and food.
- We can also see the first meeting between two outsiders and their contrasting situations: Walt, estranged from his own family and feeling alone in the midst of "his people", and Thao, who is seen as being less than a man by his own grandmother, and whose soft, insecure nature makes him an outsider in a patriarchal culture.
- On a larger scale we have here the symbolic contrast of two demographics: we see a funeral and the celebration of a birth. The older immigrant people of the neighborhood – the Polish-Americans – are dying out. The newcomers, the new immigrants from Asia, are producing babies. We see here a subtle comparison and contrasting of the past and the future of American urban demographics in the dying of one immigrant culture and the growth of the next.

Rites of passage

Rites of passage are ceremonies which mark an important stage in one's life. The blessing of the Hmong baby at the beginning of the film is one: attending a funeral is another: attending First Communion for Catholics, getting baptized in Church, graduating from school, paying taxes for the first time, going on a first date – these are all examples of rites of passage. These rituals, whether they are religious in nature or not, are always about defining where you are in society. Are you still a child? Are you a man now? Are you a girl or a woman? Do you belong to society in a dependent position – as a child – or do you now belong to society as an active, adult member and participant?

We see different examples of rites of passage in *Gran Torino*. The religious examples are very clearly defined. The process of Walt trying to "man up" Thao is a series of rites of passage for American boys: learning about how to do practical things like fix a tap in the kitchen, getting a first job, learning how to talk to another man as an equal (even if this is comically exaggerated in the film), learning how to do an honest day's work for an honest day's pay, how to ask a girl out on a date.

The Hmong gang also pressures Thao into taking part in an initiation ritual, a rite of passage which would allow him to belong to the closed society of the gang. He is supposed to steal Walt's car. This is described as an initiation (01:04:20) by Thao when he tells Walt about it.

On the DVD edition of the film there is a short documentary about masculinity and cars: in it, a car expert says "Owning a car is like a rite of passage for most men" (Leslie Kendall, curator at the Petersen Automotive Museum in Los Angeles). This idea is the meaning of the very end of the film. When we see Thao driving away in the car, we know that he is leaving the film as a man. He has been through rites of passage, taught and led by Walt, and although he comes into the story as a shy and insecure boy, he is leaving as a more mature and wiser young man.

Food

Food is a great way to bring people together. Everybody has to eat, most people like to eat, and even a bitter old traditionalist like Walt can be surprised by how good food from other cultures can be.

The opening scenes showing the Catholics and the Hmong involved in their different rituals highlight the importance of food. Walt even comments sarcastically that so many people have come to the wake because they must have heard that there was ham (00:03:45). We first see the Hmong in the form of a stream of guests and visitors bringing trays of food to the Lor house (see 00:05:05 and 00:07:50). Later, when Walt is invited by Sue into the Lor home on his birthday (00:40:20), he is very enthusiastic about their food, and the non-English speaking older Hmong women are delighted to be able feed this strange old white man. A genuine bond of generous hospitality and enjoyment is built up in this scene (00:46:00). Despite not even being able to speak the same language, Walt and the older Hmong have a good time together, made possible by the way sharing food can give people a sense of belonging together: the joy of being able to provide it and the joy of eating it. Later, when the Hmong bring him food, he does not reject it as he did earlier (see 00:25:10 and 00:52:15).

The Hmong shaman who "reads" Walt also mentions food, saying (in Sue's translation) "Your food has no flavor" (00:44:55).

Status symbols

The most important status symbol in the film is Walt's 1972 Gran Torino. A status symbol is something you display to show how you want to be identified. See below in this chapter for more on the thematic and symbolic significance of the car.

- For Walt the car is the symbol of a lost age. After the Korean War he worked in the Ford plant, a happier time for him when he understood the world, he and his wife were both young, and, as white Americans working in a booming industry, he would have felt like one of the luckiest men on the planet. It is also, as we can see in his spiteful comments about his son's Japanese car (00:08:30), a symbol for him of American supremacy.
- For his granddaughter Ashley the car is a status symbol of a different kind: it's retro chic, something cool, a vintage automobile to help her stand out in the crowd.
- For the Hmong gangsters it's just money on wheels. A vintage 1972 car in mint condition – they want Thao to steal it so they can sell it.
- Finally, for Thao at the end of the film the car has become a symbol of him becoming a man, becoming independent, and fulfilling the potential Walt wanted to see in him. As Thao finds himself he will be able to find his place in society and finally belong, no longer being an outsider in every environment.

The people who do not belong

Outsiders

The idea of belonging to something automatically raises the question of who does not belong. The two main characters in *Gran Torino* are people who do not belong – Walt and Thao are both outsiders.

Walt is too old for the world around him, in every way: his body is old and ill and dying, his attitudes and opinions are so old-fashioned they have become actively offensive, and he does not feel able or willing to compromise or adapt to new realities. Thao, on the other hand, is in a way too new for this world. He is a third-generation Asian-American, the product and symbol of a multicultural society which is still struggling to understand itself. Socially and demographically,

Walt is a remnant of a long-gone past, and Thao belongs to a future which has not fully arrived yet.

They are both also outsiders in a very real sense. Walt is alienated from his family and the world around him, which has changed beyond recognition. Thao is by nature unable to conform to either the patriarchal traditions of Hmong households or the predatory behavior of the street gangs.

These two outsiders manage to teach other and help each other grow as they expand each other's understanding of the world.

The gang members we see in the film are also outsiders, of a more extreme variety. They are actively antisocial in their behavior, and they break the law.

Walt's moral code

Walt rejects the Catholic Church and does not respect the priest, the Church or its rituals. He conforms to an outward appearance of respect:

- He glares disapprovingly at the open disrespect of his grandchildren during the funeral (00:01:00).
- He snaps at Thao "We're in mourning here" during the wake for Dorothy (00:06:45).

But when he finally goes to Father Janovich to give his confession, he appears to be mocking the priest and the act of confession (01:32:45). Despite this, however, and despite his misanthropy and racism, Walt does have a moral code. He has a number of core values. These include:

- strength and toughness
- confidence
- self-sufficiency
- manliness
- respect
- responsibility
- sacrifice

When Walt sees Thao helping the elderly woman (00:38:00), he is surprised, pleased and impressed ("Well how about that, Daisy?"). These scenes where Walt displays approval tell us a lot about his values. What he sees here in Thao's behavior is that the boy is helpful, pays attention to those around him, is not lazy, treats his elders with respect, and is at heart a good kid.

The scenes in which Walt gets Thao to work for him illustrate the importance of respect. Respect has to be earned: Walt has no respect for Thao until he has seen him working hard and facing up to his responsibilities. Thao learns through hard work to respect himself. In the world of *Gran Torino*, respect is a valuable thing which has to be earned and is not to be treated lightly.

There is a sequence of scenes during which Walt begins to teach Thao how to be a man. This progresses from learning "how guys talk" with Martin to getting a job and taking his girlfriend out on a date. Walt gives him direct advice, like: "Just look him straight in the eye and remember, a man can tell a lot by your handshake." (01:14:00). These scenes are a useful guide for understanding more about Walt's values and moral code (they also provide a satirical view of the silliness of stereotypical American "guy" stuff). Walt's moral code can be interpreted as a typical, or even stereotypical, version of old-school masculinity. These are the things a man has to know to be a man.

Masculinity

The idea of what makes a man a man is one of the film's larger themes. It applies most importantly to Thao, and the conflicting images of masculinity he is confronted with – the patriarchal pressures of the traditional Hmong community, the old-school example of Walt, and the predatory model presented by the gangsters.

It also can be seen in a couple of minor narratives, including Walt's relationship with his sons (who he thinks are lazy and spoiled), Father Janovich (the boy virgin), Walt's friends (Martin and Tim: examples of cliché "guy talk") and Sue's white boyfriend Trey (pushed around by the black men, and Walt calls him a pussy). The Hmong gang's aggression towards Thao also, significantly, has elements of emasculation.

Patriarchal Hmong culture

Thao is subject to a lot of unintentionally hurtful abuse from his family members about his uselessness as a "man". His grandmother talks about him to another relative, saying that because he does what his sister tells him to do (in this case the washing up in the kitchen) he is not a real man and won't be able to become one (00:09:20).

When Sue tells Walt that Hmong boys tend to have much greater difficulty in integrating into society than the girls, she points to a problem in Thao's life: he has no father, and no appropriate or useful male role models. His older relatives cannot speak English and are not assimilated in US society, and the younger Hmong males we see are all gangsters – sociopaths and criminals. Sue also says to Walt "It's nice of you to look after him like this. He doesn't have any real role models in his life" (01:07:00). This important scene makes it very clear how important Walt has already become to the Lor family as a kind of father figure.

Walt's example

The theme of masculinity becomes explicit following the sequence (00:50:00-01:09:00) in which Thao is working for Walt. By the end of this sequence Walt has essentially adopted the role of father figure for Thao, and has decided to make him a man – "Man you up a little bit" is how he describes his task. This is a pivotal moment in the film concerning this theme, because while the story up until this point has been about Walt being alone, with various people around him (with a significant emphasis on Sue), the focus now shifts very much to Thao and their father-son relationship. Walt has found a place to belong, a new family and a new community: and Thao has found someone who will help him make the change from boy to man.

The gang: predators

The gang are the direct opposite of Walt when it comes to their symbolic relationship to Thao. Walt is a teacher and a friend who can offer Thao a path to maturity and freedom. The gang is a nihilistic dead end of violence and exploitation.

Spider and Smokie and the other gangsters offer an example of masculinity which is defined by violence and the basic instinct to form a pack and fight other packs. When we first see the gang with Thao (00:14:00) they have just driven away the Mexicans who were harassing him. Smokie says "We just bailed your ass out, dog, get the fuck in here". Spider is also pressuring Thao to get in the car: "Get in the car [...] chill with us, man". The next time they meet (in the next scene, from 00:14:55) they are more talkative. Smokie tells Thao that he used to get beaten up a lot until he joined a gang, and now no one dares to mess with him. Spider pushes the family angle: he wants to make his "little man" cousin a real man. This scene is key to identifying and interpreting the role played by the gang in *Gran Torino*.

- For a gang, there is strength in numbers: they are not trying to recruit Thao because they think he is cool or tough, they want more people in the gang to be able to stand up better to the other ethnic gangs, like the Chicanos we have already seen.
- The issue of masculinity is for them ridiculously black and white: either you are in their gang, in which case you are a real man, or you are not, in which case you're a "pussy". Their contempt for "women's work" (Thao gardening) and the way they treat Sue (from the rudeness to the rape) shows how brutal and simplistic their view of masculinity is.
- In a twisted version of the Hmong patriarchy, Spider seems to think that as the older cousin, it is his duty or responsibility to make Thao a man. He says "You need somebody to protect you – that's what your big cousin's for [...] We're cousins, right? We're family [...] My little cousin be a little man".

The gang's concept of masculinity is in contrast to Walt's. Thao is caught between them, and this is one of the main themes in the film – the young and insecure Thao being confronted with two opposing paths for his life.

Emasculation

To emasculate means "to make a man feel that he has lost his male role or qualities"[1]. This is relevant to a lot of the language used in the film, specifically the word "pussy" (meaning coward, weakling, implying feminine qualities which are considered to be weak and un-manly).

---

[1] Oxford Advanced Learner's Dictionary, 8th edition, Oxford 2010

But two events are very intentional acts intended to emasculate Thao.

The first is when the gang ambush him and steal and break his tools. Thao has begun to work and is in many ways becoming a man, taking responsibility, earning his money, being a productive member of society. The gang are still essentially children: nasty, violent children with cars and guns, but still driven by very immature instincts. When they see Thao with his tools, they try to drag him back down to their level by destroying these symbols of his maturity and growth as a man.

The second is when they abduct and rape Sue. In the male-dominated societies we see in the film – and they are all male-dominated, from the Catholic congregation to the Hmong family and the boys' club of the gang – men are supposed to support and care for their women. They are supposed to protect them. Sue is targeted specifically because she is female: the act of rape is sexualized violence, her gender is absolutely the point of this crime. The gang is trying to provoke Thao in the most brutal way possible, by attacking his family and showing that he is not man enough to defend his own.

A man and his tools

This idea definitely belongs to Walt's old-school example of masculinity. A man must have tools, and he has to look after them and know how to use them properly. Walt's garage is filled with tools for every possible task: they are carefully organized and stored, and although Thao does not believe anyone could know what all the stuff is for, Walt knows very well which tool is needed for which job.

We see Walt softening a little towards Thao when he shows him around his garage. He is happy to buy tools for Thao later because this is, in his world, what a man needs to be a man. When Thao shows interest in what Walt has and seems to be depressed at the idea of never being able to build up a collection of tools like Walt, the old man says: "Here, take these three items right here, you can have this. WD40, vice grips, and some duct tape. Any man worth his salt can do half the household chores with just those three things. Anything else you need, you just borrow it." (01:03:30)

This is a concrete and physical step in Walt's teaching Thao to be a man. The idea of tools is very important here: life confronts you with problems to solve, and you need the right tools to do the job. In *Gran Torino*, this idea goes beyond just hammers and screwdrivers and a can of WD40. Walt's rifle belongs to this category, and so does his car. Other tools include the ability to look a man in the eye and shake his hand firmly, to be able to ask a girl out on a date, to joke around with other men to establish common ground, and to be able to ask for help when you need it and provide it when someone else needs it.

Homophobia

One other issue which should be pointed out concerning the theme of masculinity is the casual homophobia, in particular as it used between Walt and Martin. Walt also makes casually homophobic comments to Thao, and the Chicano gangsters try to provoke Thao with insults about his gender and sexuality.

This should be looked at in the same way as the racism: Walt Kowalski is probably a homophobe, just like he is actually a racist, despite everything that happens during the film. Walt often uses gendered insults. These are abusive words and phrases which use aggressively masculine language, and which suggest that females are weaker, less important and less reliable than males. For example, he often calls Thao "pussy" to suggest that the boy is weak, cowardly, unable to stand up for himself. This kind of language, though, is very similar to his theatrical racism, as discussed above. Basically, Walt likes to provoke. He likes to use politically incorrect language to offend and upset other people. This is, as the film makes clear, "how guys talk" in Walt's world.

Key scenes:

- Here are some examples of moments in the film where masculinity is an issue.
- (00:09:20) Grandma Lor: "I want my daughter to find another husband. If she married again, there would be a man in the house."
- (00:11:55) Walt calls Father Janovich a "virgin".
- (00:15:00) Fong to Thao: "What you doing, little man? Why you doing women's work?"

- (01:08:00) Sue talking to Walt: "You know, the Hmong consider gardening to be women's work."
- (00:45:00) Walt attacking Thao for not having taken his chances with Youa: "You're a big fat pussy."
- (01:09:00) Walt recommends Thao to get a job: "Of course I'll have to make a little adjustment. Man you up a little bit."

The cycle of violence

This theme is very closely connected to the religious themes because of how it is solved. One of the film's messages (statements it makes rather than ideas it explores) is that violence creates violence – violence is never an answer, it's always a question. This cycle of violence in the film runs like this:

- Thao is harassed by Chicano gangsters
- The Hmong gang drive the other gangsters away and demand Thao join them in return
- They apply pressure on Thao until he agrees to steal the car
- Walt catches Thao trying to steal his car
- The gangsters turn up at night to take Thao with them and Walt drives them off with his rifle
- The gang are seen driving by while Thao is working for Walt: they exchange menacing/insulting gestures
- The gang ambushes Thao, beats him up and steals his tools
- Walt finds their house, beats up Smokie and warns him to leave Thao alone
- The gang do a drive-by shooting at the Lor house and abduct and rape Sue
- Walt ends the cycle of violence by tricking the gang into shooting him in front of witnesses

The cycle of violence can only be broken by Walt's sacrifice. He is a man who has lived with violence for years: he was a soldier in the Korean War and has seen and done terrible things, as he tells Father Janovich (00:19:10). But despite telling the priest that he is OK with carrying the burden of what he did in the war, he is actually deeply troubled and haunted by what he did. When he sees what the cycle of violence has led to – the rape of Sue – Walt abandons his instincts to fight back, and chooses non-violence to break the cycle.

Guns, and the threat of guns

Guns are a very common feature of American cinema, and Clint Eastwood's films in particular – the largest part of his half a century as an actor has been in Westerns and violent action films. In *Gran Torino* we see guns on many occasions, but they are not often fired: the Hmong and Chicano gangsters menace each other with handguns and automatic machine pistols. Walt tries to scare Thao out of his garage with his rifle (but falls over) when the boy is trying to steal the Gran Torino. Walt scares off the gangsters with a rifle when they get in a brawl with the Lors. He also scares off the young African-American men who are harassing Sue by miming a gun, and then drawing a real gun: this very odd scene is a foreshadowing of the end of the film. It is repeated (01:01:40) when the Hmong gangsters drive down the street, evidently trying to intimidate Thao and Walt. Walt again mimes drawing a pistol and firing.

The only times we see guns actually being fired, it is the Hmong gangsters who are shooting. The first instance is the drive-by shooting on the Lor house (01:23:40) and the second is the finale, where they kill Walt (01:40:00).

The three scenes in which Walt mimes a gun are like mirror reflections of one another. In the first, Walt mimes the gun before pulling a real gun: it is a warning. In the second scene, with the Hmong, Walt's invisible gun is a reminder of how he drove them off with a real gun. In the third and final scene, Walt's mimed gun is a trap: he tricks the gangsters into shooting him in front of witnesses.

► Points to remember:

- The Hmong gangsters are the only ones we ever see actually shooting guns.
- Walt mimes shooting a gun three times: each time it has a different meaning.
- Walt has kept his old military rifle, another sign of him holding on to the past.

The rape

The rape of Sue is the crisis point in the story which changes everything. The assault on an innocent person and the awful nature of the crime are a huge step beyond what has happened so far. This act is connected to the themes of masculinity and the cycle of violence. All the people involved live in male-dominated societies and have male-dominated attitudes: the Hmong gangsters with their boys club of predators, Walt with his old-school tough guy attitude, and Thao, coming from the patriarchal Hmong culture.

Sue becomes an object or an idea which has been attacked and defiled: the gang knows this, which is why they chose this particular form of violence. The message they send is that Thao, as the man of the house, is unable to protect "his women". Walt is unable to protect his surrogate daughter. The sexual nature of this act of violence highlights Sue's identity as a female and makes it central to the crime.

The Gran Torino

An object of desire

Walt's 1972 Gran Torino is an extremely important theme in the film. Like Gatsby's extravagant yellow automobile in *The Great Gatsby*, Walt's car is an object of desire. Walt loves and worships it; Ashley covets it; the Hmong gangsters want Thao to steal it as an initiation ceremony; Tim Kennedy would love to have it. By the end of the film it has become a symbol of Thao's growth as a man, thanks to Walt's guidance and eventual sacrifice.

The car is an ambiguous symbol. Walt has it, loves it, takes care of it and admires it. But he doesn't *drive* it. When we see him in a car (00:31:10, for example) it is his beaten-up old pick-up truck. The Gran Torino is not being used as it should be: its potential is being wasted, it has become a trophy, or maybe something more sacred, like an idol or a memorial – Walt seems to worship it and what it represents (his past, and an American which no longer exists) more than actually have it in his life (by driving it and using it).

The past and the future

This is where the connection between Thao and the car becomes interesting: whereas for Walt it represents the past, what he loves and has lost (his own youth, the world he comes from, the world he understood), for Thao the car means the future, it means potential fulfilled, being given a second chance and making the most of it. The first chance is his fumbled attempt to steal the car, provoked by the gang: the second chance comes after he has apprenticed himself to Walt as a helper, basically a servant, and gradually become more of a surrogate son and a boy who is becoming a man under Walt's increasingly affectionate and caring attention. This second chance begins with Walt letting Thao borrow the car to take Youa out on a date, and ends with Thao driving the car (at the end of the film) – the first time we see the car moving, doing what it is supposed to be doing, being what it is supposed to be. The car and Thao fulfil their potential together. The car has been handed down from Walt's youth to Thao as he becomes a man. All the elements of masculinity, freedom, independence, and the almost mythological ideals of American values which the car symbolizes, are passed down from the old man who built the car to a young man from an immigrant culture for whom the car will mean something new.

Key scenes:

- (00:05:50) Ashley: "Wow, Grandpa, when did you get the vintage car?" Walt: "1972."
- (00.22.00) Walt lovingly cleaning it and admiring it after Thao tries to steal it: the car represents a lot for Walt, more than the chic vintage car Ashley wants or the trophy is represents for the Hmong gang: it's a symbol of his youth, the world he once knew, everything which has gone or is in danger of being lost.
- (01:09:10) Thao: "You made cars?" Walt: "Yeah. I put the steering column in this Gran Torino in 1972."
- (01:15:30) Tim Kennedy: "Fuck the fruitcake. How about you just hand over them keys to that Gran Torino?" Walt: "Why the hell's everyone want my car?" Kennedy: "Well, I'm not surprised."

- (01:23:00) Walt offers Thao the car to take Youa out on a date.
- (01:41:00) Thao arrives at the scene of Walt's death driving the Gran Torino.
- (01:45:15) Walt leaves the Gran Torino to Thao in his will.

The DVD special feature documentaries

The DVD and Blu-Ray editions of *Gran Torino* include two short documentaries about the car, the first of which, *Manning the Wheel*, focusses on the idea of masculinity and car culture in the USA. The second, *Gran Torino: More Than a Car* is more about US car culture than it is about the film.

Manning the Wheel has brief excerpts from interviews with the cast and crew. There are a couple of very useful quotations which can help in analyzing the film by providing some insight into what the film-makers were trying to do.

- It's not really a car picture. The car's just a symbol of a part of Walt. Walt sort of *is* the Gran Torino. He's worked on them in the factory and he's as antique as they are. (Clint Eastwood)
- It's his prize possession. He allowed himself one beautiful thing. (Nick Schenk, screenwriter)
- Owning a car is like a rite of passage for most men. (Leslie Kendall, curator at the Petersen Automotive Museum in Los Angeles)
- Generationally and culturally, Walt and Thao are able to bond when they're talking about the car [...] and that's really where they find that connection. (Robert Lorenz, producer)
- Part of Walt giving Thao his car is not giving it to his sons because they didn't earn it and he did. (Nick Schenk)

These quotations highlight a few important points. The screenwriter in particular makes it clear how important the car is to Walt, and how its symbolic value makes it so significant when he leaves it to Thao in his will. The close connection in American culture between cars and young men is emphasized in this short film, and the museum curator Leslie Kendall identifies this. The producer Robert Lorenz draws our attention to how important the car is to the relationship between Walt and Thao.

The second documentary on the DVD is less concerned with the significance of the car as a symbolic or literary device in the film, so while it can give some extra insight into US car culture and obsessions, it doesn't have much to offer when it comes to interpreting and analyzing *Gran Torino*.

Changes

Urban demographics

Immigration typically follows a pattern of integration into the majority society – this is a complex process over long periods of time, involving compromise and transformation on both sides. First-generation immigrants – the ones who came from another country, like Grandma Lor – are likely to be more closely bound to their roots and less able to adapt to their new environment. The next generation will usually be more fluent in the language and customs of their new country, having been born there, or having arrived as very young children. And the third generation – Sue and Thao – are essentially as Americans as any other American citizen. (This generational development can also be seen in the young girl who asks on behalf of her grandfather if Thao can help clean up their house 00:57:30 – she has to speak for her grandfather because he cannot speak English.) The process of change can be followed on the smallest levels – within an individual learning to adapt to a new environment – to the largest, as society changes as it takes in people from other cultures and integrates them in organic and unplanned (and unplannable) ways.

Walt may not like the way society changes, but he cannot do anything about it – except adapt himself to the new world around him. He sees his own grandchildren as being spoiled and useless, too caught up in the comfort-loving convenience of mainstream US society with its materialism and love of mass consumption. But Sue and Thao, both of the same generation as Ashley and Josh, are different. For some reason Walt is better able to deal with these two young people, apparently contradicting everything we know about him and his opinions (contempt for the young, dislike of other races/cultures).

Points to remember:

- In church at the beginning, Walt's sons talk about how Walt is "still living in the '50s" (00:01:38). A lot of what we learn about Walt suggests that this is true: he keeps his old military rifle, the medal, photos from the past, and of course his car. He seems unwilling to accept how the world around him has changed.
- Grandma Lor knows that times have changed: she complains that Walt is still there, when all the other white people have moved away. (00:10:50)

Second chances

Walt and Thao both get second chances in life. They help each other to make this happen. Thao and Sue help Walt to open up and find some new joy in life: he finds a second family, one he actually enjoys being with, and he finds new interests and projects (helping Thao become a man). He is a lonely old man who finds something new to care about at the end of his life. This caring is what helps Walt confront and overcome his guilt and the memories of the war which haunt him: his second chance at life is short and ends with his death, but it is strongly implied in the film that this sacrifice and the warm friendship he and the Lors find together are worth it.

Thao's second chance is made possible by Walt helping him discover the strength inside himself which he needs to find direction. Thao's biggest problem is that he is insecure and indecisive. He doesn't know what he wants: he only knows that he doesn't want to become a gangbanger like his cousin.

The Gran Torino is the most important symbol of this second chance.

- Firstly, it's the object he's supposed to steal as an initiation ritual, to join the gang: here it is a symbol of desire, something the gang wants, something he tries to steal. Everything about his relationship to the car here is corrupted by crime and deceit.
- And then at the end of the film, Walt gives Thao the car in his will. Thao has earned it: he didn't ask for it, greedily, like Ashley. Walt leaves Thao the car because he knows the boy has earned it, that he understands how much it meant to Walt – nothing Ashley says

suggests she has any clue how important it is to Walt – and that he will continue to treasure it as Walt did.

The car symbolizes Walt's past and Thao's future, and between those two poles it symbolizes the second chances each of these two central characters is offered in the story.

Omens

There are two scenes, very close to one another in the film, in which Walt encounters omens. The first is a newspaper horoscope, and the second is a "reading" by the Lor family shaman. Here is what they both say:

- (00:37:00) Walt reads from the newspaper: '"Your birthday today… This year you have to make a choice between two life paths. Second chances come your way. Extraordinary events culminate in what might seem to be an anti-climax. Your lucky numbers are 84, 23, 11, 78 and 99." What a load of shit.'
- (00:45:00) Sue translates the shaman's words for Walt: 'He says that people do not respect you. They don't even want to look at you. He says the way you live, your food has no flavor. You're worried about your life. You made a mistake in your past life, like a mistake that you did, you're not satisfied with. He says you have no happiness in your life, like you're not at peace.'

How relevant and important are these two omens? When we know where the story is going, we can see that they both contain truths.

The newspaper horoscope is typically vague and generalized, but "make a choice between two life paths" is relevant, "second chances" do come Walt's way, and there is an "anti-climax" of a kind following "extraordinary events". Walt has to choose how to respond to the Hmong gangsters' escalation of the violence. He has a second chance to be at peace, to be happy, to be a good father. And the extraordinary events of the cycle of violence in the conflict with the Hmong gang do in a way culminate in an anti-climax – there is no bloody revenge, no climactic shootout between the old warrior and the young gangbangers. There's an old man who tricks stupid young men into shooting him in front of witnesses: it's a climax which has its power in symbolism and long-term thinking rather than in excitement and immediate gratification.

The "lucky numbers" don't appear to be significant in any way.

The Hmong shaman's words seem to be much more personal and pointed. Walt certainly reacts very differently: he is amused and dismissive about the horoscope, but he is visibly upset and disturbed by what the shaman says. He appears to see some truth in what the shaman says. His life does lack happiness, and both his life and his food (he seems to live off beef jerky) lack flavor. But most importantly, he did make a mistake in his past, a mistake which has haunted him and because of which he can find no peace.

When watching this scene, make sure to pay attention to Walt's expressions. We can see that he sees something in the shaman's words which bothers him: he is unable to dismiss this omen as he dismisses the horoscope.

Setting and context

Gran Torino is set in the northern city of Detroit in the US state of Michigan. Many of the important themes in the film, in particular urban demographic shifts, urban decline and immigrant cultures, are particularly relevant to an important industrial city like **Detroit**.

Other topics which provide important context for an understanding of the film are the **Korean War**, the **Hmong** people, and **Catholicism** (especially the idea of confession and salvation). **Political correctness** is another issue which is important for an understanding of Walt Kowalski.

This chapter will provide brief introductions to and context for these important background topics.

Detroit, the "Motor City"

The biggest city in the state of Michigan, Detroit is famous for its historical importance as a site for manufacturing, in particular cars. Many American cities have nicknames, and Detroit's is Motor City, or Motown. The name Detroit comes from the Detroit River, which was named by the first French settlers *le Rivière de Détroit*, meaning the river of the strait (a strait is a narrow stretch of water which connects two large bodies of water).

Detroit is one of those cities which have a particular, almost mythical significance for Americans. It represents a time in America's past when the country was a leading manufacturer of cars, creating wealth for millions, pushing technology and society forward, and leading the world in a modern and powerful industry. Many of America's biggest cities have developed a similarly powerful mystique and reputation over time; for example, Los Angeles (nicknamed "the City of Angels") is the home of Hollywood and the American entertainment industry, and is associated with a culture of glamor and superficiality: New Orleans (also called "the Big Easy") is associated with decadence, voodoo and jazz: and New York, "the Big Apple", symbolizes the dynamic energy of American capitalism and the exciting potential of the American Dream. Detroit is a strong symbol of America's great industrial history, specifically, and importantly when it comes to the film *Gran Torino*, the automobile industry.

This historical and emotional meaning is important to the film, because *Gran Torino* plays against the background of the changing demographics of an industrial city in decline, and the car itself, Walt's 1972 Gran Torino, is a symbol of an older world which is now passing into history.

Detroit in pop culture: Due to its importance as a home for automobile manufacturers, Detroit was called the Motor City and also Motown. In pop culture, Detroit became famous as the home of the Motown record label, which in the 1960s and 1970s became one of the most influential and dominant forces in promoting the racial integration of pop music, creating a closer connection between the largely white world of pop and the African-American traditions of soul and R&B. Some of the most famous Motown artists include Marvin Gaye, Stevie Wonder, Aretha Franklin, Diana Ross (& the Supremes) and The Jackson Five (including Michael Jackson, whose early solo career also began on Motown).

One of the earliest of all punk bands – before the term "punk" was even being used to describe music or youth culture – was the MC5 (the Motor City 5), named after the city. At around the same time the rock singer Iggy Pop and his band The Stooges also came out of Detroit, bringing a wild and raw energy to the rock scene in the US.

Detroit has also remained famous in pop culture into the 21st century as the hometown of Eminem, the most successful rapper of all time, and the city was an important part of his autobiographical film *8 Mile*.

Key dates in the history of Detroit

1701 July 24	First trading outpost established
1802 February	Detroit officially becomes a town
1806 Sept 13	Detroit officially becomes a city: population ca. 700
1860	Population over 45 000
1870	Population over 79 000
1880	Population over 116 000
1890	Population over 205 000
1899	The Detroit Automobile Company is founded.
1900	Population over 285 000
1902	Cadillac Automobile Company begins operating
1903	Ford Motor Company begins operating
1907	First Detroit Auto Show
1910	Population over 465 000
1920	Population over 993 000
1930	Population over 1.5 million
1950	Population hits 1.85 million, the highest recorded
1963	Great March to Freedom (civil rights rally led by, among others, Dr Martin Luther King, Jr)
1970	Population 1.7 million
1972	The production year for Walt's beloved Ford Gran Torino
1980	Population 1.2 million
1990	Population just over 1 million
2010	Population just over 700 000 (this is just after Gran Torino was filmed in 2008)

Urban demographics and immigrant cultures in Detroit

Once established as a city and as a port, Detroit's population began to grow explosively. Detroit's great importance as a port and as an industrial city meant that there were jobs there. In the early 20th century the booming city (and other urban centers in the North) attracted hundreds of thousands of people from the poorer, less developed South. Most of these were African-Americans and this movement became known historically as the Great Migration. As can be seen in the timeline for Detroit above, the population of the city exploded in very short periods of time throughout its history; the Great Migration is reflected in the period 1910–1950, when the population of Detroit tripled within 20 years and continued to grow. In 1910, for example, there were around 6000 black people in Detroit, or around 1 % of the population. By 1930 there were more than 120 000, over 7 %.

This was a complex historical process, but for the purposes of providing context for the background to *Gran Torino*, what happened was that the booming industrial city attracted workers, which allowed the industries to expand even further, attracting more workers. The sudden, unplanned movement of huge numbers of new people (African-Americans from the rural American South, as well as poor Catholic immigrants from southern and eastern Europe) led to racial and social unrest.

Detroit has seen many race-related riots in its history, and it is still one of the more segregated cities in the USA – this means that there are areas or districts of the city where only one specific ethnic group lives, very often African-American (who now form over 80 % of the population). Also contributing to this process of segregation is the fact that the largely white population has long ago left the city to live in the suburbs.

The city grew incredibly fast – both in its population and its geography. By the time the decline had set in (see below) the city was huge and multi-ethnic. As businesses and manufacturers closed or left the main city, the middle-class population also began to move out to the suburbs, and Detroit itself became increasingly home to low-income populations, including ethnic minorities, among them the Hmong and other Asian migrant groups, although these still form the smallest ethnic group in the city, after blacks (over 80 %), whites (over 10 %) and Hispanics (just under 7 %).

Detroit's Asian and Asian-American population is relatively small when compared to other major American cities. The Hmong immigrants traditionally tended to live in the northeastern city districts, where there are also many immigrants from Laos, who also came to the USA following the Vietnam War and the other conflicts in Southeast Asian from the 1950s to the 1980s. The Hmong community in Detroit is one of the largest in the USA. The Hmong in Detroit are mostly poor, living in low-income housing and finding it hard to establish themselves socially and economically.

Detroit's decline

Many cities and urban areas go through periods of growth and then decline, but the fall of Detroit has been remarkable, even by American standards. Detroit's peak population was 1.85 million in 1950. In 2015 the population was just over 677,000. In 2013 the city itself had to declare bankruptcy. The single main cause for the decline of Detroit, which influenced and affected all the other causes, was deindustrialization: once the factories were gone, the jobs were gone.

Henry Ford founded the first Ford factory in Detroit in 1903. Detroit was also home to other iconic pioneers in the American car industry, including Dodge, Packard and Chrysler.

The workers in the car factories in the early days of the industry were mostly immigrants, usually from poor southern and eastern European countries like Italy or Poland. Following the chaos of the First World War and an increasingly strict and racist immigration policy in the 1920s, fewer immigrants were able to come to the USA. But the car industry was growing faster and faster, and the companies needed workers. This led to the Great Migration from the South, as Henry Ford and the others began to employ African-Americans, who hoped that life in the North would be free of the deep-rooted and widespread racism of the old South. Racial segregation continued in the North, however, and black communities were largely concentrated in specific areas within Detroit.

As well as needing workers for the factories and other physical labor (so-called "blue-collar" workers), the car industry created thousands and thousands of "white-collar" jobs. These white-collar jobs were better-paid and almost exclusively done by white people. These jobs included managers, executives, lawyers, advertisers and marketers, salesmen and so on. Following World War Two these jobs began to move out from the city center to the suburbs, and by 1960 Detroit was largely an African-American inner city surrounded by increasingly wealthy and exclusive whites-only suburban communities.

While these demographic shifts were happening, the major car manufacturers were seizing more power over the industry. The "Big Three" – Ford, Chrysler and General Motors – bought or destroyed almost all of their smaller competitors. This made the companies more powerful than ever, and it made it possible for them to fight back against labor unions and movements to establish and protect workers' rights. Unions exist to make sure that workers are treated fairly, get paid well, and are protected from being fired from their jobs for no good reason. Ford in particular, not wanting to pay its workers more money, began to decentralize its factories and manufacturing plants. This meant moving specific areas of the factories to other facilities outside Detroit. These smaller factories would have less power against the huge Ford Motor Company. It also meant that if workers went on strike to protest low pay or bad working conditions, only one small section of production would be affected. To illustrate what this meant for the workers in Detroit: the most famous Detroit production factory, at River Rouge, employed 90,000 people in 1930. By 1990 only 6000 people worked there.

Moving the big factories out of the city meant that the jobs were gone. This meant that there was suddenly less money in those neighborhoods in the inner city where the factories had once been. The people who lived there had lost their jobs, so they could not afford to buy new furniture, for example, or go out to restaurants. These neighborhoods lost retail, services and infrastructure. This led to lower property prices – the neighborhoods were suddenly poor and less attractive, so people did not want to move there. Because fewer people had jobs, fewer people were paying taxes, which made the city poorer, which meant that the infrastructure suffered – especially in the inner-city areas – and the cycle of urban decay continued.

Due to the ethnic layout of the city, with the largely African-American inner city, these developments from the 1950s onwards led to increasing crime and poverty amongst the non-white population, which in turn created even more "white flight". White flight is the phenomenon of white Americans moving away from areas of cities which are predominantly non-white. This process leads to increased economic problems in the affected areas.

In the 1970s and 1980s things became even worse for the American car industry and for Detroit. There was an oil crisis in the 1970s which led to high prices for petrol. This badly affected the car industry. In response to this, as well as for other reasons, other countries began to design and build cheaper smaller, more efficient cars. The most important countries to do this were Japan, Italy and Germany. These new kinds of cars were more attractive for consumers because they were cheaper to buy and run. American cars were traditionally big, thirsty machines which looked great but were very expensive.

In response to the oil crisis and the sudden international competition, the big American car companies began increasing automation in the manufacturing plants, using robots and automatic systems instead of human workers. They also began to cut the costs of labor even further, making the workers poorer.

These traumatic economic developments of course had social effects. From the 1970s onwards Detroit had growing problems with poverty and crime. By the 1980s it was known as America's murder capital, and in the 1980s the FBI listed it as the most dangerous city in America. Since the 1980s and 1990s, social decay and poverty in Detroit have led to large areas of the inner city being completely abandoned and becoming effectively ghost towns. This phenomenon is the background for Ryan Gosling's surreal fantasy film *Lost River* (2014).

Points to remember:

- Detroit used to be an important industrial center, but it has been in decline for many years now.
- As in all big cities, demographic changes since the 1950s have led to great changes in neighborhoods. Detroit was always an effectively racially-segregated city.
- Detroit is an important and emotional symbol for a lost era of American wealth and power (specifically connected to the automobile industry).

Korean War

The Korean War was fought from 25 June 1950 to 27 July 1953 between North Korea, with the support of China and the Soviet Union, and South Korea, aided by the USA. It began when North Korea invaded the South and ended with the signing of an armistice. An armistice is an agreement to stop fighting: it is not the same as a peace agreement. The two Korean states are still officially at war with one another in 2018, although recent developments suggest that this technical state of war may soon be ended.

The country of Korea was divided into two parts during the Cold War following World War Two, with the Communist states of China and Soviet Russia influencing the North, and the South being helped by America and the West. Following the damage caused by American bombing during the Korean War, the North was basically destroyed as an industrial society. South Korea went through some difficult times after the war. A very unpopular authoritarian regime was in power immediately after the war and was supported by the USA. South Korean governments have often been accused of being corrupt, and the country has a history of anti-American opinions and movements, to a greater or lesser extent depending on the social climate.

One concrete result of the Korean War which is relevant to *Gran Torino* was the Immigration Act of 1965, which was passed by American lawmakers and allowed more people of different races and nationalities to apply for American citizenship. The huge numbers of American-Korean mixed-race children born as a result of the American soldiers being stationed in South Korea created a problem for South Korea: Korean society is traditionally very concerned with racial purity, and mixed-race children or fatherless children are not easily accepted. Walt refers to this when talking to Sue: he complains about her having a white boyfriend, saying "You shouldn't be hanging out with him. You should be hanging out with your own people" (00:35:15). Koreans and mixed-race Koreans became the fastest-growing part of the Asian immigrant population in the USA. This first generation would have been the generation of Grandmother Lor and the older Hmong we see in the film. They are not well assimilated into American society – they cannot speak English and they continue to live according to the traditions of their homeland. The younger generations have adapted to their new home – Sue Lor and Thao are as American as any other teenager.

Walt Kowalski fought in the Korean War. He saw terrible things happen (00:19:10) and Father Janovich believes that Walt feels guilty because of the things he did, which indeed he does (00:28:10 and 01:36:30). He still has guns and medals from his time as a soldier. He says that his racism towards Asians was influenced by his experiences during the war (00:24:10). He talks about how his experiences in the war taught him to react quickly and violently to critical situations (00:27:50). The fact that he is a war veteran is important when looking at Walt Kowalski as a character. The things he did during the Korean War haunt him all his life and explain why he has such a dark and angry personality.

▶ Points to remember:

- The Korean War (1950–1953) was between the North (supported by Communist states) and the South (supported by the USA and the United Nations).
- Walt served in the Korean War: he saw atrocities and killed enemy soldiers.
- American soldiers were stationed in Korea and there was a lot of inter-marrying, and thousands of children of mixed race were born.
- American immigration laws were changed to make it easier for Korean and Korean-American people to become US citizens.
- America is home to the second largest population of Koreans outside Korea (the largest is in China).

The Hmong

Despite all the Korean War talk and Walt's anti-Korean racism, the Hmong are not from Korea. As Sue explains to him (00:35:30), the Hmong people are from "different parts of Laos, Thailand and China". She tells him that the Hmong fought on the side of the Americans during the Vietnam War (1955–1975) and were afterwards persecuted by the Communists from North Vietnam. She says that the Hmong were brought to the USA by the Lutherans, a Protestant branch of Christianity.

Sue has to explain a lot to Walt about Hmong (see the scene in the car, 00:35:00) and how they interact with one another (00:42:00). His ignorance at the barbecue she invites him to gives her the opportunity to explain – and we the viewers the opportunity to learn – more about who the Hmong are.

Hmong-Americans

During the Vietnam War the Communist North Vietnamese invaded the Kingdom of Laos in 1975. The Hmong were persecuted and hunted down and were driven into refugee camps on the border to Thailand. Many thousands died. The US initially granted around 3000 Hmong asylum as refugees: by the end of the 1970s about 30,000 Hmong had been allowed to come to America.

Hmong-Americans take their surnames from the traditional clans they belong to. So Walt's neighbors are called Lor, which comes from the clan name Lauj.

According to the 2010 US census there are a little over 260,000 Hmong in America. About 4000 live in Detroit. The largest Hmong population is in the Minnesota-St Paul-Bloomington area, with over 74,000.

The Hmong face quite serious problems in their communities in America. Many of these problems come from the strict gender roles expected by their traditional society, and, among older generations, by the fact that these are a traditionally rural, agricultural people with no historical experience of education or industrial, consumerist societies.

A census conducted in the USA in 2000 found that 60% of Hmong over the age of 24 do not have education beyond high-school level. 40% of Hmong drop out of school, a 2013 study showed. This lack of education is, of course, a big problem in a modern society like the USA. A lack of education in one generation is also often a problem for the next generation.

Hmong traditions have proved to be a problem when adapting to US society. Girls are expected to be obedient and to marry – their accepted and expected role is wife and mother. The pressure on Hmong girls and women to conform is intense and damaging. It is a patriarchal (male-dominated) society and women are subject to misogyny. We see this in *Gran Torino* with the contempt that is shown for "women's work" by Grandma Lor as well as by Spider.

The situation for boys is also not good. They under pressure to support their families, but also to maintain cultural traditions and customs. These pressures lead many to rebel (for example, by joining gangs) or to simply give up in one way or another. Sue points out to Walt that Hmong boys often end up in jail, and when she talks about her dead father she describes a man who was more concerned with preserving strict traditions than loving his children. Hmong-Americans are among the poorest ethnic groups in the USA. They have the highest rate of mental health disorders (over 33%) among all Asian groups.

Points to remember:

- Sue and Thao belong to the Hmong ethnic group. They are the grandchildren of immigrants who fled persecution in Southeast Asia following the war in Vietnam.
- The Hmong are an ethnic group which is not specific to one country in Southeast Asia.
- They try to hold onto their traditions and culture even in later immigrant generations, even though these traditions are a source of serious economic and health problems for their communities.

Catholicism

Walt's dead wife Dorothy was a devout Catholic, and she had made the young priest promise to take Walt's confession after she was gone. Walt has little time for religion or for priests and he is unfriendly and rude to Father Janovich.

Walt may not be religious, but religious ideas do play a role in *Gran Torino*. Here is a brief introduction to the most important concepts related to Catholicism which appear in the film.

The following words and phrases related to the Catholic Church and Catholic rituals are relevant to the film:

Confession

Confession is the act of telling a priest about the bad things you have done, in the hope of being forgiven. The Catholic Church organizes sins in different categories, depending on how important they are, and the priest can tell the sinner to perform certain actions to show that they regret having done what they did and are ready to receive forgiveness (these actions are called penance). For minor sins, for example, penance may be to say ten Hail Marys (see below). The ritual of confession is shown in the film (01:33:00).

Congregation

The group of people gathered to worship God, usually in a church. The congregation is led by the priest.

Shepherd, flock, sheep

When Father Janovich finds Walt in the bar with his friends (00:17:20) he says "So here's where my flock congregates when they're not in church." A flock is the correct name for a group of sheep. The use of sheep-related phrases in Christianity goes back to its origins. One of the many names or titles for Jesus in ancient Church tradition is *Agnus dei*, a Latin phrase meaning "lamb of God" which is used repeatedly in the Latin Catholic Mass ritual. A famous Psalm (number 23 – the Psalms are poem-like books in the Bible) begins with the line "The Lord is my shepherd". Other books in the Bible refer to Jesus as "the Good Shepherd", and the Gospel of John has one entire chapter (book 10) which is devoted to sheep and shepherd symbolism and imagery.

Two points here are relevant to *Gran Torino*. Firstly, the lamb is a symbol of gentleness and innocence, but above all it is a symbol of sacrifice. In ancient cultures lambs were valuable possessions, and a sacrifice is always measured by its value to the person making the sacrifice: Do they really mean what they say, or are they just posing? How much are they willing to give up, to literally sacrifice, in support of their prayers? The sacrifice of a lamb was a worthy, meaningful act. The concept of sacrifice is very important to *Gran Torino* as Walt sacrifices himself at the end to save Thao, avenge Sue, and remove the dangerous threat of the Hmong gang.

This symbolism can, however, be used to mock and ridicule Christians. Sheep are not exciting or cool animals: they tend to be fairly stupid, and they lack courage and individuality. They are used by humans mostly for wool, and we do not have the kind of connection to sheep that we have to dogs or horses, for example, animals which we generally respect and with which we often have genuine emotional relationships. In comparison to other animals which are a part of our lives, sheep lack personality and attractiveness, and they have no qualities which we as humans tend to admire or want to copy. So a Catholic like Father Janovich is an easy target for a man like Walt who wants to mock him and his beliefs, when he calls his congregation "sheep" in a dismissive and insulting way: "Why don't you go tend to some of your other ... *sheep*." (00:07:15).

Salvation

Salvation means to be saved. It is the most important idea in Christianity, and it is also important in many other religions. For Catholics and other Christians, salvation is only possible through the belief in Jesus Christ. Catholics believe that people are born in "original sin", and that the only way to escape the punishment for sin (which is to go to Hell after death) is through belief in Christ.

Walt is not a Christian: he does not believe that Jesus was the Son of God and that he died for his sins. He mocks Father Janovich's idea that "death is bittersweet – bitter in its pain, sweet in the salvation" (00:18:50). But Walt's sacrifice at the end of the film is also his salvation: he sacrifices himself to save Thao and Sue. But he has also found a way to make his death mean something, and in doing so, to balance the bad things he has done, specifically the murder in Korea of a young soldier who wanted to surrender. This event has haunted him, and Walt carries the burden of it like a sin. But because he does not respect the Church or the ritual of confession, he chooses to atone for this great sin in his own way, to find his own salvation.

Seminary

Walt dismisses Father Janovich as being a young man just out of the seminary. A seminary is a school for priests.

Devout

This adjective describes someone who has strong faith, who really believes in their religion and who follows its rituals and customs. Dorothy was devout: Walt is not.

Priest

The priest is the leader of the congregation in the Catholic Church. The priest interprets the Bible and the faith itself for the believers, acts as a spiritual leader, and is ideally also involved in the community to help those in need. A Catholic priest is an authority figure, and as the representative of God on Earth, is a very important person for devout Catholics.

Hail Mary / Our Father

Also known as the *Ave Maria* (in Latin), the Hail Mary is a prayer Catholics use to ask the Blessed Virgin Mary, the mother of Jesus, for help or support in their lives. Our Father is also known as the Lord's Prayer (it is called *Vater Unser* in German). In the Bible (Matthew 6:9 and Luke 11:2) Jesus teaches his followers this prayer. Father Janovich tells Walt in response to his confession to "say ten Hail Marys and five Our Fathers" (01:34:00).

Political correctness

There are very intense debates in Western societies about the issue of free speech versus the alleged restrictions of political correctness. This debate has been going on for quite some time now, and while it is often reduced to a left-right political opposition, things are, as usual, more complicated than they seem.

Political correctness (PC) is "the principle of avoiding language and behaviour that may offend particular groups of people"[1]. This obviously includes not using racial slurs to describe people of a particular ethnicity – *Gran Torino* has plenty of examples. The roots of PC lie in the awareness that the demographic which has for so long dominated social discourse and culture – white heterosexual men – is not the only demographic with a right to an opinion. The essential idea of political correctness is that it is neither good nor correct to assume that there is a "normal" standard against which everything else is measured and found to be funny, weird, wrong or less important. This has to do with identity and exclusion.

Walt sees himself as an American: this is his identity. He belongs to an idea of white America and makes fun of individuals who do not belong to this group or share this identity. Walt, as a straight white man, behaves as if anything which does not belong to his social group – American, white, male – is strange and somehow open for mockery or abuse. He enjoys voicing non-PC opinions to provoke. Sometimes this works out fine, as with his teasing banter with both Sue and Martin.

Walt's theatrical racism, the film seems to argue, is just banter – it is just provocative talk from an old man. It is up to the individual viewer to decide if this effort works, to make the casual racism seem less harmful: the more we get to see Walt grow as a person through the film, the more we are told and shown that he is not a bad man, he just has a non-PC sense of humor and way of expressing himself.

This problem is one small part of *Gran Torino* and only applies to Walt's more theatrical expressions of his very real racism. But while his impatience with people being overly-sensitive may be relatable, it is

---

1 The Oxford Advanced Learner's Dictionary, 8th edition, Oxford 2010

worth remembering that people who are repeatedly subjected to real abuse may not share his delight in the provocative use of racist insults.

Written test

At some point while working with *Gran Torino*, you may have to do a written test. What the test looks like depends to some extent on the *Bundesland* you are in. The following model exam is based on the type of written examination used in Baden-Württemberg. The article examines the city of Detroit just after the time in which the film was set, in which its decline accelerated even more rapidly, following the financial crisis of 2008.

Test

Text

From: Paul Harris, *the Guardian*, 1 November 2009.

How Detroit, the Motor City, turned into a ghost town

Try telling Brother Jerry Smith that the recession in America has ended. As scores of people queued up last week at the soup kitchen which the Capuchin friar helps run in Detroit, the celebrations on Wall Street in New York seemed from another world.

The hungry and needy come from miles around to get a free healthy meal. Though the East Detroit neighbourhood the soup kitchen serves has had it tough for decades, the recession has seen almost any hope for anyone getting a job evaporate. Neither is there any sign that jobs might come back soon.

[…] Outside his office the hungry, the homeless and the poor crowded around tables. […] This is an area where times are so tough that the soup kitchen is a major employer for the neighbourhood, keeping its own staff out of poverty. But now Brother Jerry fears he may also have to start laying people off.

Officially, America is on the up. The economy grew by 3.5 % in the past quarter. On Wall Street, stocks are rising again. The banks – rescued wholesale by taxpayers' money last year – are posting billions of dollars of profits. Thousands of bankers and financiers are wetting their lips at the prospect of enormous bonuses, often matching or exceeding those of pre-crash times. The financial sector is lobbying successfully to fight government attempts to regulate it. The wealthy are beginning to snap up property again, pushing prices up. In New York's fashionable West Village a senior banker recently splurged $10m on a single apartment, sending shivers of delight through the city's property brokers.

But for tens of millions of Americans such things seem irrelevant. Across the country lay-offs are continuing. Indeed, jobless rates are expected to rise for the rest of 2009 and perhaps beyond. Unemployment in America stands at 9.8%. But that headline figure, massaged by bureaucrats, does not include many categories of the jobless. Another, broader official measure, which includes those such as the long-term jobless who have given up job-seeking and workers who can only find piecemeal part-time work, tells another story. That figure stands at 17%.

[...] In the months to come, no matter what happens on the booming stock market, hundreds of thousands of Americans are likely to lose their homes.

For them the recession is far from over. It rages on like a forest fire, burning through jobs, savings and homes. It will serve to exacerbate a long-term trend towards deepening inequality in America. Real wages in the US stagnated in the 1970s and have barely risen since, despite rising living costs. The gap between the average American worker and high-paid chief executives has widened and widened. The richest 1% of Americans have more financial wealth than the bottom 95%. It seems the American hope of a steady job, producing rising income and a home in the suburbs, has evaporated for many. A generation of aspiring middle-class homeowners have been wiped out by the recession. "Poor people just don't have the political clout to lobby and get what they need in the way Wall Street does," said Brother Jerry.

There is little doubt that Detroit is ground zero for the parts of America that are still suffering. The city that was once one of the wealthiest in America is a decrepit, often surreal landscape of urban decline. It was once one of the greatest cities in the world. The birthplace of the American car industry, it boasted factories that at one time produced cars shipped over the globe. Its downtown was studded with architectural gems, and by the 1950s it boasted the highest median income and highest rate of home ownership of any major American city. Culturally it gave birth to Motown Records, named in homage to Detroit's status as "Motor City".

Decades of white flight, coupled with the collapse of its manufacturing base, especially in its world-famous auto industry, have brought the city to its knees. Half a century ago it was still dubbed the "arsenal of democracy" and boasted almost two million citizens, making it the fourth-largest in America. Now that number has shrunk to 900,000.

Its once proud suburbs now contain row after row of burnt-out houses. Empty factories and apartment buildings haunt the landscape, stripped bare by scavengers. Now almost a third of Detroit – covering a swath of land the size of San Francisco – has been abandoned. Tall grasses, shrubs and urban farms have sprung up in what were once stalwart working-class suburbs. Even downtown, one ruined skyscraper sprouts a pair of trees growing from the rubble.

[…] The brutal truth, some experts say, is that Detroit is being left behind – and it is not alone. In cities across America a collapsed manufacturing base has been further damaged by the recession and has led to conditions of dire unemployment and the creation of an underclass. Richard Feldman, a former Detroit car-worker and union official turned social activist, sees disaster across the country. Sitting in a downtown Detroit bar, he lists a grim roll call of cities across America where decline is hitting hard and where the official end of the recession will make little difference. […] The economic changes going on, he believes, are a profound de-industrialisation with which America is failing to come to terms.

"We are going to have to face the end of the industrial age," he said. "This didn't just happen last October either. It's been happening here in Detroit since the 1980s. Detroit just got it first, but it could happen anywhere now."

Annotations

1 recession: *wirtschaftlicher Abschwung* **3** Capuchin friar: *Mönch des Kapuzinerordens* **8** evaporate: *verfliegen* **14** lay sb. off: *jdn. entlassen* **23** splurge: spend a lot of money **39** exacerbate sth.: make sth. worse **48** clout: influence **67** scavenger: *Plünderer/in.* **70** stalwart: *tapfer, loyal*

Teil I: Comprehension

1 Choose the correct answer. Indicate the line(s) and give a quote.
The neighbourhood in East Detroit has …

A recovered very well from the recession.
B been in trouble for decades.
C been the cause for celebrations on Wall Street.
D always needed a soup kitchen.

2 Choose whether the following statement is true or false. Indicate the line(s) and give a quote.
The recession may have been over by 2009, but the banks in America were still struggling at the time this article was written.

3 Choose whether the following statement is true or false. Indicate the line(s) and give a quote.
Different estimates of the rate of people without work in America for this period in 2009 range from just over 9 % to 17 %.

4 Choose the correct answer. Indicate the line(s) and give a quote.
The long-term effects of the recession following the financial crash of 2008 include:

A The triumphant return of the automobile industry to America's northern cities.
B A slow but steady increase in wages to make up for the higher cost of living.
C An increase in the inequality between the richest and the poorest people in America.
D Lower salaries for top executives and an end to multi-million dollar bonuses for bosses.

5 Which two of the following sentences characterize the city of Detroit? Indicate the line(s) and give a quote.
A It was one of the first cities to experience the troubles which now affect so much of America following the recession.
B Detroit was a surreal place in full decline, but it has recovered well since the 1950s.
C The city was once upon a time one of the wealthiest and most successful industrial cities in the world.
D Detroit became nicknamed Motown in the 1980s thanks to the great success of the automobile industry and the Tamla Motown record label.

6 Fill in the gap with a word from the text. Indicate the line.
Detroit was a great industrial city, and during the Second World War (1939–1945) it was called the __________ of democracy.

7 Fill in the gap with information from the text. Indicate the line.
The USA seems unable to come to terms with ___________.

Teil II: Analysis

Describe two or three examples of characters, ideas or images from the film *Gran Torino* which illustrate points made in the article?

Teil III: Writing

Choose *one* of the following:
1 The soup kitchen mentioned in the article is an example of food and religion being combined. Discuss the role of food and rituals in *Gran Torino* as signs of belonging and identity.
2 The text describes the changes that have affected the city of Detroit. Examine Walt's sense of identity in the changing landscape of Detroit.

Dealing with the tasks

Teil I: Reading comprehension

The example questions given here use some of the exercise formats you will be used to by now, and which you will also encounter in exams: multiple choices, true/false, and gap filling. These exercise formats are designed to check that you have understood the language and the content of a text. The sequence of the exercises usually follows the order in which the information can be found in the text: the first question will refer to a section near the beginning, and the final question to something near the end of the text. If you read both the text and the wording of the questions carefully, you will find these reading comprehension questions to be quite easy. Get used to skimming paragraphs to look for key words, and remember that you can almost always find the meaning of an unfamiliar word of phrase through its context – that is, by thinking about the language and information surrounding it.

Solutions

1 B
2 False. In the article it says that the banks are once again making billions of dollars in profit ("The banks [...] are posting billions of dollars of profits", ll. 16–18)
3 True. The lower figure is the official, optimistic statistic. More realistic figures are much higher, and include the number of people who have part-time work which is not enough to live on. "Unemployment in America stands at 9.8 %. But that headline figure, massaged by bureaucrats, does not include many categories of the jobless. Another, broader official measure, which includes those such as the long-term jobless who have given up job-seeking and workers who can only find piecemeal part-time work, tells another story. That figure stands at 17 %." (ll. 28–34)
4 C. "The gap between the average American worker and high-paid chief executives has widened and widened. The richest 1 % of Americans have more financial wealth than the bottom 95 %." (ll. 42–44)
5 A: "There is little doubt that Detroit is ground zero for the parts of America that are still suffering." (ll. 50–51)

C: "The city that was once one of the wealthiest in America is a decrepit, often surreal landscape of urban decline. It was once one of the greatest cities in the world. The birthplace of the American car industry, it boasted factories that at one time produced cars shipped over the globe." (ll. 51–55)

6 arsenal (l. 62)

7 a profound de-industrialisation (l. 81)

Teil II: Analysis

Think about how these concrete, specific issues concerning the decay of Detroit since its glory days in the 1950s might be relevant to the film. Do any characters represent something the article talks about? Do any scenes in the film illustrate the sense of decay and depression that has struck Detroit, and which has become worse since the financial crash of 2008?

Here are some examples of items from the film which illustrate points made in the article:

- The character of Walt, an old man who once had a good job at the Ford car factory. Walt very clearly represents the long-lost economic boom times of Detroit, before different factors combined to result in the **de-industrialisation** of the city, destroying jobs and leaving the city with a fraction of its earlier population.
- Walt's son Mitch sells foreign cars. Walt complains about this, Mitch himself complains about his father's racist attitudes, but beneath the racism and the glorification of American-made cars is the economic truth that cheaper, more effective foreign-made cars essentially put the big old American car factories out of business. The issue is complex and emotional for those directly affected by it but the **economic facts are hard and cold**.
- The film shows us the daily reality of **urban decline** without making a big deal of it. We never see crowds of people or busy streets in the film. During the scene when Walt saves Sue from being harassed by the young men, the surrounding area is literally an urban wasteland. The houses are falling apart (Walt gets Thao to repair the house opposite his own). We never see thriving shopping streets, busy highways, crowds of young people, or any of the

"bright lights, big city" visuals so often used in US cinema to emphasise the size and vibrancy of American urban centres.

- Detroit is shown in *Gran Torino* as a ghost town: what we see are a few old people blowing around between the porch, church and the barber shop, and aimless, hopeless young immigrant men prowling empty streets looking for trouble.

Teil III: Writing

Task 1: The first question requires you to consider how rituals and food contribute to the sense of belonging. It is recommended you look at pp. 89–91of this book, which examine the role of ritual and food in the film.

Task 2: The second question revolves around identity. You are asked to examine how Walt feels as the community he knows disappears and is replaced with another community.

Here, you need to examine how he views his Hmong neighbors at the beginning of the film, how gangs are now evident on the streets of the city, how immigrants from non-European and non-Christian backgrounds are now prevalent (scene in the doctor's office). It is important to stress Walt's suspicion of these newcomers compared to his happy banter with his barber Martin, who comes from a European Catholic background.

However, while the article emphasizes the negative side of white flight, Walt is an example of a white person who comes to terms with his changing surroundings and contributes to the lives of the immigrant community, albeit with some reluctance at first.

A brief glossary of cinematic terms

Camera angle

The angle at which the camera is pointed at what it's looking at: from below, from above, or from an angle.

Cut

Putting two different shots together. There are different ways to make a cut, each of which creates a different impression and has a different effect.

- Cross-cut (quickly cutting back and forth between two different scenes to create suspense and tension, for example in the scene In the garage where Walt surprises Thao trying to steal the car).
- Jump cut (an abrupt and rapid cut from one scene to another, usually intended to shock or startle the viewer. This is a relatively extreme technique, like suddenly shouting at someone, so it isn't used very often, most commonly in horror films).
- Continuity cut (the most common kind of edit, a smooth and logical movement from one scene to another, expressing continuity in the narrative).

Diegesis

Everything which happens within the world of the film. Music playing on a radio we can see in the picture, the second hand on a clock ticking on camera, two characters having a conversation: these are all diegetic elements. The rap music we hear in *Gran Torino* is diegetic: it is coming from a source within the fictional world of the film (car radios, for example). The music we hear during the scenes in which Walt is watching Thao work on the house across the road is non-diegetic: it is not *within* the world of the film – the characters can't hear it – it is outside this fictional world, it is only there for us, the viewers.

Directing

The director of a film is responsible for using the available tools (actors, cameras, technical crew) to make real his or her vision of the screenplay. A director has an idea of how the film should feel, the impression it should make, how the story should be told, and directs everyone involved in front of and behind the camera to make sure this idea becomes reality.

Editing

The arrangement of camera shots to tell the story. Typically, film narratives are told in sections (scenes) of sequential edits (shots). It can help to think of editing as being like grammar and punctuation in a text: when does a sentence end, and how does it end? With a sudden exclamation (!) or with a puzzling fade-out ...

Framing

How the visual elements within a shot are arranged within the picture. This includes how big something is made to look within the camera eye and what kind of angle the camera takes to what it's looking at. For example, when Walt appears on the lawn to break up the fight between Thao and Sue and the Hmong gang, the camera looks at him from a low angle, and he appears to fill the screen. These two factors make him appear very powerful: the camera makes him look huge and the perspective (filmed from below) increases this impression. Framing is a very important element of cinema, and it can tell us a lot about what is going on in the scene in question – it is as important, in a way, as dialogue.

Montage

Editing apparently unrelated scenes together to create a new impression: basically, A and B are edited together to create something new in C. This "something new" is usually, in mainstream cinema, going to be the passing of time. The key montage in *Gran Torino* is the scene where Walt watches Thao working for him. The editing suggests that time is passing. Instead of us having to watch literally days of Thao repairing gutters and mowing lawns, we are told by the editing of different scenes that this is what he has been doing.

Mise-en-scene

This phrase is French, and it means "placing on stage". It refers to literally everything that is placed in front of the camera – actors, settings, props, costumes, lighting – everything.

Scene

A unit of film narration. Like a verse in a poem or a chapter in a novel, a scene is a unit which is a part of a greater whole. The opening of *Gran Torino*, in the church at Dorothy's funeral, is an example of a scene: when we are taken to Walt's house for the wake, the scene has ended and a new scene begins.

Shot

If a film can be compared to a book, then scenes are like chapters and shots are like sentences. They can be long and rich in detail, or short and punchy. Technically, a shot is the continuous footage between two edits.

Take

One version of a shot. A director may shoot several takes of a shot to find the best one. This is equivalent to the writer correcting his or her words: rewriting a sentence or a paragraph to make it better, or sometimes just changing one single word.